Exam success in

CW01514671

Andy Ford

Distilling six years of experience as Chief Examiner, Paul Humphreys answers all the questions commonly asked by students and teachers, discusses what questions can be set and how the student should prepare for the exam, and explores the keys to success. This book is an essential purchase for every candidate and particularly for those who want to raise the grade they attain.

Paul Humphreys is Reviser for AEB A-level Psychology and Senior Lecturer in Psychology at University College Worcester. He is an editor of the A-level journal, *Psychology Review*, and was Chief Examiner for AEB A-level Psychology from 1992 to 1997.

Routledge Modular Psychology

Series editors: Cara Flanagan is the Assessor for the Associated Examining Board (AEB) and an experienced A-level author. Kevin Silber is Senior Lecturer in Psychology at Staffordshire University. Both are A-level examiners in the UK.

The *Routledge Modular Psychology* series is a completely new approach to introductory level psychology, tailor-made to the new modular style of teaching. Each short book covers a topic in more detail than any large text-book can, allowing teacher and student to select material exactly to suit any particular course or project.

The books have been written especially for those students new to higher-level study, whether at school, college or university. They include specially designed features to help with technique, such as a model essay at an average level with an examiner's comments to show how extra marks can be gained. The authors are all examiners and teachers at the introductory level.

The *Routledge Modular Psychology* texts are all user-friendly and accessible and include the following features:

- sample essays with specialist commentary to show how to achieve a higher grade
- chapter summaries to assist with revision
- progress and review exercises
- glossary of key terms
- summaries of key research
- further reading to stimulate ongoing study and research
- website addresses for additional information
- cross-referencing to other books in the series

Also available in this series (titles listed by syllabus section):

ATYPICAL DEVELOPMENT AND ABNORMAL BEHAVIOUR

Psychopathology
John D. Stirling and Jonathan S.E. Hellewell

Therapeutic Approaches in Psychology
Susan Cave

BIO-PSYCHOLOGY

Cortical Functions
John Stirling (forthcoming)

The Physiological Basis of Behaviour: Neural and hormonal processes
Kevin Silber

States of Awareness
Evie Bentley (forthcoming)

COGNITIVE PSYCHOLOGY

Memory and Forgetting
John Henderson

Perception: Theory, development and organisation
Paul Rookes and Jane Willson (forthcoming)

COMPARATIVE PSYCHOLOGY

Reproductive Strategies
John Gammon (forthcoming)

DEVELOPMENTAL PSYCHOLOGY

Cognitive Development
David Cohen (forthcoming)

Early Socialisation: Sociability and attachment
Cara Flanagan (forthcoming)

PERSPECTIVES AND RESEARCH

Controversies in Psychology
Philip Banyard

Ethical Issues in Psychology
Mike Cardwell (forthcoming)

Introducing Research and Data in Psychology: A guide to methods and analysis
Ann Searle

SOCIAL PSYCHOLOGY

Social Influences
Kevin Wren (forthcoming)

Interpersonal Relationships
Diana Dwyer (forthcoming)

OTHER TITLES

Health Psychology
Anthony Curtis (forthcoming)

Sport Psychology
Matt Jarvis (forthcoming)

Exam success in AEB psychology

Paul Humphreys

London and New York

First published 1999
by Routledge
11 New Fetter Lane, London EC4P 4EE

Simultaneously published in the USA and Canada
by Routledge
29 West 35th Street, New York, NY 10001

©1999 Paul Humphreys

Typeset in Times by Routledge
Printed and bound in Great Britain by Clays Ltd, St Ives plc

All rights reserved. No part of this book may be reprinted or
reproduced or utilised in any form or by any electronic, mechanical,
or other means, now known or hereafter invented, including
photocopying and recording, or in any information storage or
retrieval system, without permission in writing from the publishers.

British Library Cataloguing in Publication Data
A catalogue record for this book is available from the British Library

ISBN 0–415–19092–4

To Dee, my partner,
who makes all things possible

Contents

Acknowledgements

Paul Humphreys and Routledge acknowledge the Associated Examining Board (AEB) for granting permission to use their examination material. The AEB do not accept responsibility for the answers or examiner comment in Chapter 6 of this book or any other book in the series.

The exam paper

Introduction

Let us begin this book with what I trust will be most welcome news to those of you who have bought it to help you get the grade which you need in the AEB A-level and AS-level examination papers.

There is a very limited number of questions which the examiners are allowed to set.

Without compromising my professional integrity – or even worse, getting fired by the examining board – I will share with you the 'rules of the game' which all AEB Psychology examiners have to adhere to.

We will consider in detail the documents, such as the syllabus content and the so-called Glossary of Terms, which the question-setters use, and I will show you what are and what are not legitimate questions for your psychology course. In Appendix B at the back of the book I have provided you with an extensive list of possible questions. Whilst I cannot pretend that the list given is the complete list of all possible questions which could ever be set – the examining board *would* fire me for trying to do that (and examiners are always capable of springing the odd surprise, even while observing the tight rules and restraints within which they operate) – I am confident that most of the angles are covered. This has both an up and a down side. On the positive side it should increase your confidence to know that the questions which can be set are limited and predictable (and, perhaps more importantly, you can rehearse how you would deal with them in the comfort of your own home!). The negative aspect is that it may tempt you to learn, off-by-heart, a series of plans or model answers to each set of questions. I will return to this point in a later chapter, but for the moment let me just say that the preparation and reproduction of what we call Blue Peter answers ('here is one I made earlier') is not a good examination strategy. There are many reasons for this. Most importantly they encourage rote-learning at the expense of genuine understanding.

Let us now begin our exploration of the factors that determine which questions can legitimately appear on your examinations papers, and which cannot.

rule 1: ONE ANSWER, TWO SKILLS – skills A and B are equally weighted

All questions set on the AEB Psychology syllabus – with the single exception of those set on Research Methods (modular 7), more of this shortly – require the examination candidate – YOU! – to demonstrate two separate skills. Furthermore in *all* questions these are equally weighted, 12 marks out of 24 for each. These two skills are named, rather unadventurously, Skill A and Skill B.

Skill A

The Skill A requirements are for you to show:

* knowledge and
* understanding

This knowledge and understanding will be of the following aspects of psychology (AEB 0675/0975 syllabus, 2000):

* theories
* concepts
* studies

2

- methods
- applications
- ethical responsibilities of researchers
- major issues and controversies
- individual, social and cultural diversity

So we have a specified list of content and an identification of two skills which you will need to apply to specified content items (don't worry, no question is going to ask you to address more than two or three items on the list above!).

We may think of Skill A as descriptive 'narrative', like telling a friend the storyline of the film you saw last night (you know, who did what, to whom, with what outcomes and so on).

Let's take a psychology example. If you were required to 'Skill A' one *theory* of Cognitive psychology (Developmental Psychology section of the syllabus, sub-section 6.2) and chose to focus upon the work of Jean Piaget, you could focus on the development of schemata, the functional invariants of accommodation, assimilation and equilibration, and the stages and sub-stages of cognitive development and the characteristic abilities of the child at these stages of development. Alternatively, you may be asked to focus upon his *research studies* – what did he do? who were his participants? what were his methods? what did he find? Finally (syllabus 6.2) you may be required to consider *applications* of his work to education – for example, classroom practices.

The important point to make is that all of these are vehicles for you to show your *knowledge and understanding* of Piaget's psychology. The examiner is giving you the means of demonstrating your knowledge.

Skill B

So what about Skill B? We may think of it as 'commentary'. Let me illustrate what I mean by going back to our earlier analogy of the film conversation with your friend. If you begin to appraise the film ('that part was really scary because…'; 'the use of music added such a lot to the film…') or to interpret the film ('it seems to me that the message was "you never get away with lying about two-timing"') you are clearly moving beyond the descriptive level of just 'saying what happened'. A sports commentator will be displaying both of these skills. He or she will not only be describing to us what is happening but will be offering *evaluation* ('the difference between confidence and panic in the Argentinian defence was always Michael Owen'), *analysis* ('France have had 72 per cent of possession so far but have managed only three shots on target') and *interpretation* (all that heavy stuff on tactics).

To get back to psychology (mercifully, if you're not a football fan!), Skill B requires you to demonstrate the following skills to the same specific content areas listed above for Skill A:

- analysis
- evaluation
- critical awareness
- interpretation

Okay, so having identified what the skills are, how do you know which ones are being demanded in any particular exam question? Easy – you need to know your *injunctions*.

rule 2: USING THE INJUNCTIONS

A little earlier I mentioned the Glossary of Terms. This document, published by the AEB, gives definitions of the 'action words' (technically, injunctions) used in exam questions. These tell you whether you should be 'Skill A-ing' and/or 'Skill B-ing'.

There are only sixteen of these so let's get specific:

Skill A-only injunctions
Consider; define; describe; examine; explain; outline; state

Skill B-only injunctions
Analyse (or critically analyse); assess (or critically assess); criticise; evaluate (or critically evaluate); justify

Skill A and Skill B injunctions
Compare and contrast; critically consider; distinguish between; discuss

Once you have learned which terms go where, test yourself by writing each injunction out on a slip of paper and then put each into one of three piles (A-only; B-only; A and B). Why bother? Well, if a question asks you to *describe* two theories of perception (syllabus 5.1) and you offer *commentary* – for example by evaluating the theories – you will receive no credit whatsoever for your answer from the examiner. This may sound tough but what the question-setters are trying to do is to let you know exactly what they want from you. You shouldn't have to have Mystic Meg qualities to do well in this exam!

The bare minimum you need to know is the above list.

I said the list above is the minimum you need to know. Let's go one better and look at the definitions of the injunctions which the Board provide.

consider	demonstration of knowledge and understanding of topic
define	explanation of what is meant by a particular term
describe	presentation of your knowledge of the topic
examine	presentation of a detailed, descriptive consideration of the topic
explain	conveyance of your understanding of topic, which should be coherent and intelligible
outline/state	summary description of topic in brief form
analyse	demonstration of understanding through consideration of the components or elements of the topic
assess	informed judgement/considered appraisal of how good or effective something is (based on an awareness of strengths *and* limitations of information/argument presented)
criticise	critical appraisal/evaluation of strengths *and* weaknesses of topic

evaluate	informed judgement regarding the value of the topic (based on systematic analysis and examination)
justify	consideration of the grounds for a decision (e.g. by offering a supportive consideration of the logic behind a particular interpretation)
compare/contrast	consideration of similarities and/or differences between topic areas (this may involve critical consideration of points of similarity *and* differentiation)
critically consider	as 'consider' (above), but additionally an awareness of the strengths *and* weaknesses of the material presented
distinguish between	demonstration of differences between topic areas at both descriptive and critical levels of contrasting
discuss	description and evaluation by reference to different if not contrasting points of view

I accept that this is fine detail stuff, but it will enable you to know *exactly* what the question-setter wants from you. For example, compare the Skill B-only injunctions 'assess' and 'justify'. Take a moment to re-read these carefully.

I hope it will be obvious that whereas 'assess' requires you to look at both sides of an issue ('strengths and limitations'), 'justify' requires you to offer only 'a supportive consideration'. Look also at 'examine' and 'outline': although both are Skill A-only, the former requires 'detailed descriptive consideration', the latter 'a summary description'.

Some of you may be familiar with the line from a song which goes

> It ain't what you do
> It's the way that you do it.
> That's what gets results.

The same principle is certainly true here.

(Just in case I've lost you: it's not just the amount of psychology that you know, it's knowing what to do with it – describe it, evaluate it etc. – that counts.)

rule 3: USING THE SYLLABUS WORDING

The question-setters are strongly encouraged to use the exact wording from the syllabus wherever possible in the questions they set. Let's look at some examples taken from recent exam papers (with thanks to the AEB for allowing us to use them):

Syllabus wording	Exam question
4.1 theories and research relating to the causes and effects of emotional and behavioural problems in childhood and adolescence, e.g., attention-deficit hyperactivity disorder, autism and developmental dyslexia.	Describe and evaluate research into any two emotional or behavioural problems in childhood (e.g., attention-deficit hyperactivity disorder; autism; developmental dyslexia). (24 marks) [January 1997]
6.1 theories and research into the effects of enrichment and deprivation on the child.	Describe and evaluate studies of the effects of enrichment and/or deprivation on the child. (24 marks) [January 1997]
1.2 effects of interpersonal relationships, e.g. on happiness and mental health.	Discuss some of the effects that interpersonal relationships have been shown to have on a person's psychological well-being (e.g., happiness and health). (24 marks) [June 1997]
3.4 physiological and non-physiological theories of motivation and emotion.	(a) Describe and evaluate one physiological theory of motivation (12 marks) (b) Describe and evaluate one non-physiological theory of motivation (12 marks) [January 1998]

7.2 controversial applications of psychological research, which should include advertising, propaganda and warfare, and psychometric testing (including personality and intelligence testing)	Discuss why the assessment of personality by means of psychometric tests might be considered a controversial application of psychology (24 marks) [June 1998]

I would not wish to give you the impression that the wording is *always* taken straight from the syllabus, but even when it is not you will find that it is simply the same topic or area merely re-worded somewhat or that the question *derives out* of the syllabus wording. Examples are given below.

Syllabus wording   **Exam question**

2.3 explanations of the use of different signalling systems in non-human animals, e.g. communication in marine mammals	(a) Consider the use of two different signalling systems in non-human animals. (12 marks) (b) Assess the advantages and disadvantages of these two signalling systems. (12 marks) [June 1997]
5.1 perceptual organisation (space, movement, pattern recognition, perceptual constancies and illusions)	Describe and evaluate any two theories of pattern recognition in relation to visual perception. (24 marks) [January 1997]

Note that in the first example part (b) is not literally stated in the syllabus wording, but certainly should have been covered as part of the Skill B preparation for this topic. In the second example, the term 'theories' is not specified in the syllabus wording but, in covering the nature of those examples of perceptual organisation (including pattern recognition), it is reasonable to expect that students will know about theories as well as research evidence.

What we can deduce from this is that sometimes the links between the syllabus wording and the questions may be *implicit*, but on the majority of occasions the link will be literal and *explicit*.

The lesson to be learned here is that you need to know the syllabus – intimately! What you see there is what you are likely to get on your examination paper.

rule 4: ONE QUESTION PER SUB-SECTION

The current AEB A-level psychology syllabus comprises eight sections, each divided into sub-sections as below:

1 Social Psychology
   (1) Social cognition; (2) Social relationships; (3) Social influence; (4) Pro- and anti-social behaviour
2 Comparative Psychology
   (1) Evolutionary determinants of behaviour; (2) Reproductive strategies; (3) Kinship and social behaviour; (4) Behaviour analysis
3 Bio-psychology
   (1) Basic neural and hormonal processes and their influence on behaviour; (2) Cortical functions; (3) Awareness; (4) Motivation, emotion and stress
4 Atypical Development and Abnormal Behaviour
   (1) Atypical development; (2) Conceptions and models of abnormality; (3) Psychopathology; (4) Therapeutic approaches
5 Cognitive Psychology
   (1) Perceptual processes; (2) Attention and performance limitations; (3) Memory; (4) Language and thought
6 Developmental Psychology
   (1) Early socialisation; (2) Cognitive development; (3) Social behaviour and diversity in development; (4) Adolescence, adulthood and old age
7 Perspectives
   (1) Approaches to psychology; (2) Controversies in psychology; (3) Ethical issues in psychology
8 Research Methods in Psychology
   (1) Nature of psychological enquiry; (2) Design and implementation of experimental and non-experimental investigations; (3) Data analysis

The numbering system I have been using when describing parts of the syllabus should now be clear: for example, 6.2 refers to the Cognitive development sub-section (number two) of the Developmental Psychology section (number six).

The key thing for you to know is that, with the single exception of the Research Methods section, the AEB guarantee that a question will be set to every sub-section of the syllabus.

In Appendix A at the back of this book I have dissected the syllabus, sub-section by sub-section so you can see at a glance exactly what you will be required to cover for the sub-sections that you concentrate on for the exam.

Let me first of all explain how the tables 'work'. I'll use the Pro- and anti-social behaviour (sub-section 1.4 of the syllabus) table as an illustration:

Activity/ process	Content	Specific focus	Including	For example
explanations; research studies	altruism; bystander behaviour			
social psychological theories	aggression			social learning theory; social construc- tionism
implications of research	aggression	reduction and control of aggressive behaviour		
	pro- and anti- social behaviour	media influences		
explanations	pro- and anti- social behaviour	individual, social, cultural diversity		

The second column – I'll deal with the first a little later – is 'Content' and this identifies the main topic areas. In this case we have five:

- altruism
- bystander behaviour
- aggression
- pro-social behaviour
- anti-social behaviour

The layout makes it clear that altruism and bystander behaviour are 'bunched together' as are pro- and anti-social behaviour. What this means in practice is that questions could focus upon either or both. For example:

> Critically consider psychological explanations of altruism. (24 marks)
> Describe and evaluate psychological explanations of bystander behaviour. (24 marks)
> Discuss psychological explanations of altruism and bystander behaviour. (24 marks)

The third column – 'Specific focus' – narrows the point in question. So, for example, two aspects of pro- and anti-social behaviour are focused on: media influences on pro- and anti-social behaviour, and individual, social and cultural diversity in pro- and anti-social behaviour.

The fourth and fifth columns are even more specific. The syllabus sometimes specifies a topic and adds 'including…'. There are none of these in the Pro- and anti-social behaviour sub-section of the syllabus so look at the one on Social influence (page 77). Here we see that the content area of Social power has two 'includings': leadership and followership; Collective behaviour also has two: crowds and mob behaviour.

Returning to the Pro- and anti-social behaviour sub-section, we can see that aggression has two 'For examples': social learning theory and social constructionism. The reason I have allocated two columns for the 'includes' and 'examples' is because of rule 5.

rule 5: 'INCLUDINGS' ARE PRESCRIPTIVE, 'FOR EXAMPLES' ARE ILLUSTRATIVE

Remember our task: we are building up a definitive statement which will enable you to know exactly which questions can legitimately appear on your exam papers.

Where the syllabus gives 'includings' these are fair-game for exam questions, 'for examples' are not.

The reasoning behind this is that the includings are there to guide you to certain specific aspects of a topic which you will be expected to have covered (leadership as a form of social power would be one, as we have just seen); the examples are there merely to be helpful and give you some ideas.

The only way that examples can be included in the wording of an exam question is *as* just an example. For instance:

Discuss social-psychological theories of aggression (for example, SLT; social constructionism). (24 marks)

In this case you can concentrate on the examples given in the question or you can choose to ignore them completely. What power! In the above example you could, quite legitimately, address de-individuation and group-norm theory instead of the ones named. Not so for the includings. If these are given in the question you *must* focus upon them. They can also be the focus of questions in their own right, for instance:

Discuss psychological research into leadership. (24 marks)

Conversely,

Compare and contrast SLT and social constructionism as theories of aggression. (24 marks)

could never appear on an exam paper (as they are only given as examples).

To summarise:

Includes are 'must-do's; for examples are 'may-do's.

The specific focus

All four columns we have looked at so far are concerned with content (or psychological topics, if you prefer). But we have one last thing to consider – *how* it is being addressed. For example, are we concerned with theories or research, definitions or applications? If we take the example of aggression, examiners would expect very different essays if they asked you to write about the nature of aggression as opposed to discussing empirical research into aggression. Consequently, this constitutes the final 'aspect' of the question formation.

I have headed the first column 'Activity/process' to indicate it is what the psychologist is 'doing to' the topic (for example, carrying out research; developing theories; applying what we know to a particular area of interest or concern).

The AEB Glossary of Terms identifies and defines the following as key terms.

Term	Definition
applications	actual or possible ways of using psychological knowledge in an applied/practical setting
concepts	an idea or group of ideas, often the basic units of a model or theory
evidence	material (empirical or theoretical) which may be used to support or contradict an argument or theory
findings	the outcome or product of research
insights	perceptions which facilitate an understanding or conceptual reappraisal
methods	different ways in which empirical research is and may be carried out
model	often used interchangeably with 'theory', but less complex/elaborate and often comprising a single idea or image meant as a metaphor; explanation is often by analogy
research	the process of gaining knowledge and understanding via either theory construction, examination or empirical data collection
studies	empirical investigations providing evidence which,

through reference to investigator's name and/or details of investigation/outcome, should be recognisable to the examiner

theory   a (usually) complex set of interrelated ideas/principles intended to explain or account for certain observed phenomena

You should make a point of reading these terms carefully and perhaps making notes to help you really 'get your head around them'. Whereas most of the definitions will come as no surprise to you, a few may. For example, research – which a lot of students would regard as 'doing a study', is defined as this ('empirical data collection') but also as constructing and examining *theories.*

As Michael Caine once observed, 'Not a lot of people know that…'.

Progress exercise

Let's put all of this to the test.

Look back to the *Pro- and anti-social behaviour* table, and let's see if we can begin to identify the questions which the examiners can legitimately set.

They can ask you about:

1 either theories or research studies on altruism and/or bystander behaviour
2 social-psychological theories of aggression
3 the implications of aggression research for its reduction and/or control
4 media influences on pro- and/or anti-social behaviour
5 explanations of pro- and/or anti-social behaviour addressing individual/social/cultural diversity

Now let's check out the questions which have been set so far and see if they fit with the list above.

January 1997
(a) Outline and evaluate two psychological theories of aggression. (12 marks)
(b) Critically consider how research on aggression may contribute to its reduction. (12 marks)

June 1997
Critically consider the view that the media may exert a pro-social influence. (24 marks)

January 1998
A specific question was given and candidates were required to describe and assess the contention that social-psychological explanations of aggression are adequate. (24 marks)

June 1998
Describe and evaluate psychological research relating to human altruism and/or bystander behaviour. (24 marks)

Do they fit? Yes they do!
January 1997 clearly comes from item 2; June 1997 from item 4; January 1998 from item 2 (again) and June 1998 from item 1.
I hope this shows you that the questions are fair, limited in number and largely predictable.

Legitimate exam questions

The list given in Appendix B at the back of this book, as I said at the outset, is not a full, definitive list covering every single possibility, but it should cover most of them. The main reason why a definitive list could not be written can be seen in the two January questions above, the parted question and the quote/discuss question. Examiners can demonstrate their ingenuity in both of these areas. In the first one this is achieved by dividing up topics in such a way as to make very specific demands, rather than placing general demands upon you. I suppose all the inter-combinations *could* be worked out but the number would be large and it would be impractical for you to 'learn', say, thirty answers to cover each possible question area. It is much better to be able to cover all the general angles and then be adaptable/flexible in how you apply these on the day (according to the specific demands of the question).

rule 6: THE USE OF PARTED AND QUOTE/DISCUSS QUESTIONS

Although not a hard-and-fast rule like the ones we have considered so far, this is certainly a strong guideline. It is *highly likely* that each sub-section of the exam will contain at least one parted question and that each module paper will contain at least one quote/discuss question. What is unknowable, of course, is where they will 'fall'. There are, however, some things I can tell you about these questions which will help you prepare for them.

As we shall see in Chapter 3, the marking scheme which will be used to mark your exam papers is divided into six bands for both Skill A and Skill B. Because of this, most parted questions tend to be in multiple units of 6 marks. The most common splits are 12/12; 6/18 and 6/6/12, but a 6/6/6/6 would be possible. Have a look now for examples of these splits in Appendix B at the back of the book.

It is important to remember that Skills A and B are equally weighted (rule 1), 12 marks each (apart from the Research Methods section as we shall see at the end of this chapter). In Chapter 2 we will look in detail at how parted questions are constructed and how you should deal with them, but let me for the moment simply note that the marks allocated to the parts should give you a clear signal about how to 'weight' your answer. For example, when questions such as:

(a) Outline one theory of cognitive development. (6 marks)
(b) Discuss applications of this theory to education (for example classroom practices). (18 marks)

appear on exam papers, it is not uncommon for candidates to write several pages answering part (a) – generally vastly detailed accounts of Piaget's theory and work – and a couple of sketchy paragraphs or less for part (b). I hardly need to point out that the first part of the question is only carrying a quarter of the overall marks, so you can imagine what the consequences would be for these candidates.

One final point on parted questions for the moment: when answering these you *must* divide your answer to reflect what you see on the exam paper in front of you. If you write a general answer the examiner is obliged to separate it out on your behalf but it is almost certain that your general answer will under-emphasise certain important aspects addressed by the parted question (such as application to education in the example above) and include a good deal which is irrelevant in this specific context.

'Quote/discuss' questions

The so-called 'quote/discuss' questions began appearing on AEB A-level psychology papers in 1992 and have appeared on every paper since then (generally one per module these days). Let's consider an example:

> "The improvement claimed by psychotherapists after treatment [is] no more or less extensive than that found without any treatment at all…Considerable improvement occurs…simply with the passage of time." (H.J. Eysenck, 1957)
> Discuss.   [June 1993]

Just in case you're not familiar with the conventions of using quotations, let me point out that the '…' simply indicates that something has been cut from the original at this point, usually in the interests of brevity or of joining together different points made by the writer. Conversely, words in square brackets have been added to the original, usually because of a change in grammatical construction. The essential point is that as far as you are concerned you can simply ignore these as being 'technicalities'.

From what students have told me in the past, I know that many of you systematically avoid these questions, perhaps because they are perceived as 'difficult' or because there is an unjustifiable view that the time spent reading and dissecting the quotation is time wasted. The truth of the matter is that candidates do at least as well if not better on the quote/discuss questions than on the 'conventional' essay questions. I think there are two reasons for this. First, the quotation can act as, at the least, a pointer to direct you to consider certain issues. With the longer quotations, they can be almost be regarded as mini-plans for your answers. I think the second advantage of these questions is that they dissuade students from reproducing their Blue Peter answers, and these answers are almost always inappropriate. As I shall emphasise later, if you want to do well in the exam you must always answer the question on the paper rather than the one in your heart.

Let me summarise my advice to you concerning quote/discuss questions.

- Don't make a policy decision to avoid them – they can help you by directing your answer.
- Always make full use of the quotation and make a point of addressing all the points contained within it.
- Ensure that at least somewhere in your answer you *explicitly* make a reference to the quotation, even if it's just 'as it says in the quotation given in the question....' (Failure to do this is likely to result in your answer being precluded from the top two mark-bands for Skill B, so effectively your answer will be marked out of 20 instead of 24, and those marks may well be the difference between a grade.)
- Always pay careful attention to the instruction(s) given after the quotation. It may be just a general invitation to discuss (as above) or it may be much more specific as below:

'Linguistic determinism is the claim that language strongly influences the way a person thinks or perceives the world.'
Discuss ways in which social and/or cultural variations in language may influence thought.   [January 1998]

One final point: I'm sometimes asked if it matters whether or not you are already familiar with the quotation. The answer – no it doesn't. Many of them will have been made up specifically for the exam anyway (you can easily identify these because they have no name accredited to them on the paper and they are set in single rather than double quotation marks).

rule 7: SPECIFYING HOW MANY

In most of the exam questions which focus upon research or theories you will be told how many you should include, for example:

Describe and evaluate any two theories of hypnosis. (24 marks)
[June 1997]

The reason for being so specific is, once again, to let you know exactly what we want from you, rather than you having to dust off your crystal ball. Sometimes, however, the examiners want to let you decide whether to focus on a small number of studies/theories or to write a broader answer dealing with a larger number. This is achieved by using the phrase 'x or more' such as:

Critically consider one or more explanation(s) of the organisation of information in memory. (24 marks)

or leaving it open-ended, such as:

Describe and evaluate psychological research into the development of sociability and/or attachments in early childhood. (24 marks)

[both June 1998]

This raises the issue of *breadth versus depth*. Clearly if you chose to offer just one explanation in answering the memory question above (quite legitimate, of course, given the wording of the question), it would be reasonable to expect that the examiner marking your paper would expect far more depth, elaboration and sophistication than if you had offered, say, four or five. This is what examiners call the depth/breadth trade-off.

A student once asked me about an extreme case scenario when she inquired how low would the depth and sophistication requirement be if you sketched out a dozen or more explanations?! The answer is, if the argument was followed to its logical conclusion, an absurdly large number of explanations would result in sub-A-level standard expectations, so we have to impose a common-sense constraint and talk about breadth/depth trade-off having to be consistent with the performance we expect at A-level.

My advice to you is that in preparing for the exam you should know two or three theories or studies in real depth. For example, in the case of a study, what the researcher was investigating, sample size and 'nature' of participants [for example, whether they were American students, as is often the case], what was done in the study, what results were obtained, how were these analysed and interpreted, and all the Skill B critical/evaluative stuff. In addition you would also need to know about a much larger number of theories/studies for which you can offer brief thumb-nail sketches. Do remember, though, that this applies only to questions which have an unspecified number (n). What happens in a question where there is a specified n and you ignore it? Whether you have given too many or too few, it's bad news.

The 'too many' scenario. If a question specifies that you cover two theories, for example, and you give three, the examiner will mark all of them but will only credit the best two. There is one interesting exception to this. If you can convince the examiner that, in answering an 'n=2' question, a third theory is being used as part of the evaluation or appraisal of one of the two 'legitimate' theories, the examiner will allow it. But you must make a good and explicit case in the body of your answer; if you don't, the examiner will not credit the extra study or studies.

The 'too few' scenario. If you are asked for two and offer one, or three and offer two, you will – to use examiner-talk again – be 'partially performing'. The bad news is that you will lose access to one-third of the available marks because both Skill A and Skill B will be marked out of 8 instead of 12. I'm sure I don't need to spell out the consequences of this.

rule 8 : THE RESEARCH METHODS SECTION IS COMPLETELY DIFFERENT

This section of the syllabus is not bound by the majority of the rules which constrain the question-setters in all the other sections. Let's run through the differences so that you know exactly where you stand. They can be summarised as follows:

- You must answer all the questions (and all their parts) on the exam paper. For once there is no choice!
- The examining board doesn't specify the number of questions which can be set here. To date it has been two, but it could be one or three (or more!). The only constraint is that a total of 24 marks is available.
- The format of the questions is not specified (I will return to this later).
- The usual division (explicit and 50/50) between Skill A and Skill B does not apply here.

- Following on from the previous point, the injunctions used in these questions are not tied to those given in the Glossary of Terms. You can be asked to 'state', 'name', 'identify', be suggestive(!) and so on. Just look at the number of marks allocated to the questions and take it from there.
- The focus point of the question can be on any part of the whole syllabus (social, developmental, comparative, etc.).This is because the section is viewed as *synoptic*, i.e. an overview of the whole syllabus.

Tackling the questions

All of this may sound a little frightening, but if you bear in mind the following points there won't be any problems for you:

- Attempt all parts of the question – even if the answer doesn't immediately seem apparent to you it can almost always be deduced through a careful analysis of the stimulus material given in the question itself which you should always endeavour to work with. Remember it is there for a purpose. If everything else fails, guess – you've got nothing to lose!
- Bear in mind the notion of 'marks worth' – a question allocated 1 mark is not demanding as much of you as one allocated 4 marks.
- Unlike everywhere else in the exam, 'positive marking' is not employed. What does this mean? Positive marking means that only that which you write and is correct is noted, any errors, mistakes, faux pas (however, hilarious!) are disregarded by the examiner. The logic behind this is that you will have wasted precious time in delivering these, so any penalty would be a double whammy. This doesn't apply in Research Methods because the questions can often be answered in a single phrase, so almost no time is lost. Therefore if you are asked what is the appropriate test to analyse the data given, you won't be granted the luxury of being able to list every one you know, with the examiner checking along the list to find the right one!
- As elsewhere in the exam, quality of language (see Chapter 4) is assessed so you are strongly advised to write in full sentences (for example, 'An appropriate test to analyse these data is the Mann–Whitney U-test', not simply 'Mann–Whitney'.

- No mathematical computation requirements can be made, but you do need to be able to 'read' tables (such as those given for significance).
- Be clear about the differences between the Research Methods section of the syllabus and requirements for your coursework. They are different – check them out. The logical sequence of the Research Methods syllabus is *planning/doing/analysing-interpreting*.

So what is predictable about the Research Methods questions?

Having spent all this time telling you that this section is significantly less predictable than all the others, the good news is that I can identify the styles of questions which have been set so far. With one exception, discussed at the end of the section, they fall fairly neatly into the following categories:

1   *The vignette*. There is a short account of a hypothetical study (usually only one paragraph long) followed by a series of short-answer questions (such as 'state a null hypothesis for this study'). The history of these questions to date is:

> *January 1997*: a laboratory experiment on memory. Six questions worth 2 marks and one question worth 1 mark. Total: 13 marks.
> *June 1997*: a field experiment on effectiveness of therapy. Six questions worth 2 marks and one question worth 1 mark. Total: 13 marks.
> *January 1998*: a study on eating behaviour comparing the laboratory experiment with naturalistic observation. Two questions worth 4 marks. Total: 8 marks.
> *January 1998* (second question): content analysis of sex differences in television advertisements. Two questions worth 3 marks and five questions worth 2 marks. Total: 16 marks.
> *June 1998*: naturalistic observation study of play in infant school children. Two questions worth 4 marks. Total: 8 marks.

2   *Minimal study with data presentation.* The focus in these ques-
    tions is largely upon interpreting data ascribed to a hypothetical
    study (which is generally summarised in a few lines).

    June 1997: Spearman's rho; scattergrams; significance table.
    One question worth 4 marks, three questions worth 2 marks
    and one question worth 1 mark. Total: 11 marks.

3   *Context-free questions.* Unlike styles 1 and 2, the questions here
    are 'free-standing', i.e. unrelated to text (e.g. What is meant by a
    case study? Give one advantage and one disadvantage of the case
    study method).

    January 1997: the case study. Two questions worth four
    marks, one question worth 2 marks and one question worth
    1 mark. Total: 11 marks.

The second question on the June 1998 exam was a mixture of styles 1
and 3. A laboratory-type experiment concerned with the impact of
prior knowledge on time estimation; data analysis by bar chart and
Mann–Whitney U test. One question worth 3 marks, six questions
worth 2 marks and one question worth 1 mark. Total: 16 marks.

You now know what can come up on your paper.

Let's spend a little while in Chapter 2 looking at common student
myths, fallacies and downright inaccuracies. By the end of this you
will also know just what won't be coming up!

Summary

- The questions that can be set on the exam paper must satisfy
  certain rules or constraints.
- Questions are equally weighted between two Skills, A and B.
- The Skills can be identified by examining the injunctions used in
  the question (e.g. 'describe' as opposed to 'evaluate').
- Some injunctions (such as define) are Skill A only, some (such as
  justify) are Skill B only and others (such as discuss) require you to
  demonstrate both.

- The wording of most of the questions is very similar to that given in the syllabus.
- With the exception of the Research Methods section, there is a guarantee that one question is set to each sub-section of the syllabus. An analysis of the syllabus is given as Appendix A in this book.
- Where the syllabus uses the term 'including', the topic can form part of a question; where it uses 'for example', it cannot form part of a question (other than as mere suggestion or guidance).
- The outcomes of psychological 'work' (such as models, research, theories) are referred to in very exact ways in questions. Definitions are given above on page 13.
- Considerable use is made of parted questions. Due to the nature of the marking scheme, parts tend to be in units of 6 marks (e.g. 6/18; 12/12; 6/6/12).
- Some questions include quotations which you should make reference to in your answer.
- In questions where a number (e.g. of theories or studies) is not specified, there can be a breadth/depth trade-off.
- Questions set for the Research Methods section of the exam do not have to adhere to the above constraints.[*]
- A large number of illustrative questions is given as Appendix B in this book.

---

[*] See Ann Searle's book, *Introducing Research and Data in Psychology*, in this series for further help on the Research Methods section of the examination.

2

The banana skins of the psychology exam

A couple of summers ago I was passing the time of day chatting to some students at a sixth form college where they had just sat an A-level psychology examination. I asked one particular student what she thought of it. She looked rather sheepishly at the floor and said that it had been fine apart from 'the Piaget question' (student shorthand for the Cognitive development sub-section of Developmental Psychology). I was thrown by this as I thought this had been a perfectly straightforward question which would be very popular. Her next remark made everything clear to me:

'It was set last year – it shouldn't have come up this time!'

I shouldn't have been surprised, because this is one of a whole number of widely held misconceptions about the nature of the exam papers that one hears all the time. And just in case you are wondering, they come from teachers as well as students!

Let me now take the opportunity of finally putting these misconceptions to rest; after all it is just as important to know what you can't be asked to do as to know what you can (so that you won't waste your time anticipating and preparing for things which aren't going to happen).

I'll run through them quite quickly but by the end I'm sure you will feel better informed and more confident.

MYTH 1: year-on-year patterns

This is clearly the one which had floored the poor student mentioned above (as well as her mates, I must add). There seems to be a widely held belief that examiners work to set patterns. Quite what these patterns exactly are is rarely, if ever, articulated, but the myth seems to incorporate at least two principles:

- if it came up on the previous paper, it won't come up on the current one
- if a banker topic (see Myth 2 below) hasn't turned up for a while, it's more than likely that it will be on this paper

Let me be quite categorical here: both of these are just plain wrong. I'm reminded of the commentator on the National Lottery draw who informs us, with mounting excitement as the draw progresses (even though for almost all of us the excitement *decreases* with each consecutive ball!) that that particular ball has appeared x times in the last y months, z times as the bonus ball. So what?! If there are fifty balls in the machine each has an equal one-in-fifty chance of being drawn in every draw.

Now I'm not going to pretend that the selection of topics by the question-setters is entirely random – we *do* look at tables which show the pattern of topics 'coming up' on past papers, but we tend only to do this after the questions have been set, almost as a final thought. There are certainly no patterns that we work to – we merely note that one particular topic hasn't come up for a while or that another has cropped up quite frequently, and bear that in mind (along with lots of other factors) for the next round of question-setting. So please don't waste your time trying to discern patterns from past papers: you'll be wasting your time as such patterns don't exist. Or if, on the odd occasion, they do this was entirely unintentional on our part!

The above myth is part of the general exercise of *question-spotting*. Let's look at another facet of this extremely risky and ill-advised process.

MYTH 2: banker topics

'Some parts of the syllabus are so important that they are much more likely to come up than others. Some are so marginal you can effectively forget them.'

Wrong!

Again I'm not sure what the exact formula is here, it often comes in different versions. Let me illustrate it by reference to 'the Milgram answer'.

We examiners know that however a question on obedience to authority is worded (even if half of it focuses on implications for our understanding of independent behaviour as occurred in June 1997), or however a question on ethics is phrased, we will receive hundreds and hundreds of replications of *the* Milgram answer: believe me, it is *the* Milgram answer – almost identical descriptive detail, same order, same evaluation. Even the same joke ('Milgram was shocked by his results…'). What is truly distressing is that when obedience doesn't come up and the ethics question is entirely Milgram-unfriendly, for example on research with non-human animals, the DSM (Desperately Seeking Milgram) candidates will still, frantically, endeavour to find a home for the Milgram answer – perhaps aggression, perhaps relationships, perhaps leadership, perhaps anything really. This must be because these candidates believe that Milgram is such a banker topic that a question paper without him is inconceivable. I suspect there are three reasons behind this:

- Milgram's work on obedience was vastly important and influential – indisputably true, but surely this cannot be used as a justifiable reason to include it on every single exam.
- It's inherently interesting (and – yes – shocking!) – fair enough, but so is a lot of the rest of psychology and surely we cannot ignore all the research which for whatever reasons just doesn't grab the headlines. Academia isn't always theatre.
- It takes up a lot of space in the textbooks. No, sorry – I may have grudgingly acknowledged aspects of the other two but not this one. Exam questions are set to the syllabus, not to specific textbooks. For example, individual, social and cultural diversity is specified in many parts of the syllabus and yet is not extensively addressed in many of the textbooks used by A-level students. Just

because textbook writers dedicate large amounts of words to the Milgram obedience studies doesn't influence the likelihood of exam coverage a jot. Tough, but there we are, I thought you should know. The other side of the coin is equally as important: just because any particular textbook only minimally covers a syllabus topic (or even has nothing on it), doesn't make it a 'marginal' topic as far as the exam is concerned. It just means that, sadly, you've got some information-gathering to do.

Let us look at an example. On page 10 I noted that the Pro- and anti-social behaviour sub-section of the syllabus (1.4) contained five areas:

1   Explanations and/or research studies: altruism and/or bystander behaviour.
2   Social psychological theories: aggression.
3   Implications of aggression research for reduction and control of aggression.
4   Media influences on pro and/or anti social behaviour.
5   Individual, social and cultural diversity in pro- and/or anti-social behaviour.

The key point I must emphasise here is that in planning for your examination you must work on the assumption that each of these items has a one-in-five chance of coming up every year. No single one of them is more or less likely than any other, for whatever reason.

MYTH 3: the wording of the questions doesn't really matter

'A good, general answer in the area will earn plenty of credit.'
    Completely wrong again.
    Questions could not matter more – they are the exact requirement being made of you by the examiner. This shouldn't be off-putting – it should be seen in a wholly positive and supportive context where you are being given all the information you need. I can promise you that if you put into practice all the advice that is given between the covers of this book, the exam will enable you to show what you know and can do, rather than being something to be suspicious and fearful of.
    In Chapter 3 we will explore how you can train yourself to dissect questions and know exactly what they want from you. But before we

do that, I want to spend a little time working through the following exercise which links the importance of the wording of the questions with the rules for question-setting discussed in Chapter 1.

In the next chapter, we move on to a discussion of how you can learn to read analytically and 'unpack' the exam questions on your paper.

'The wrong questions'

All of the following questions could *not* be set on an AEB Psychology exam paper. Putting into practice all that you have learned so far, jot down on a piece on paper *why* you think each one is inadmissible. As well as refreshing your memory on the rules of the game (Chapter 1), you will need to look at the syllabus synopsis (Appendix A). The answers are given below.

1   Distinguish between the fundamental attribution error and self-serving bias within attribution theory. (24 marks)

2   What are the effects of interpersonal relationships, for example on happiness and mental health? (24 marks)

3 (a) Describe one theory of conformity. (12 marks)
   (b) Assess the anti-social influences of the media. (12 marks)

4 (a) Describe procedures used in classical conditioning. (12 marks)
   (b) Analyse the contribution of Pavlov's work to psychology. (12 marks)

5   Consider research which has been carried out into the effects of drugs on behaviour. (24 marks)

6 (a) Outline what is meant by stress. (12 marks)
   (b) Describe one piece of research on stress. (6 marks)
   (c) Evaluate this piece of research. (6 marks)

7   Describe and critically evaluate one or more physiological theories of motivation and two non-physiological theories of emotion. (24 marks)

8   Discuss the assumptions of the medical, behavioural, cognitive, humanistic and psychodynamic models of abnormal psychology, including their implications for treatment and ethical implications. (24 marks)

Review exercise

9   Criticise therapeutic work that has been carried using ECT and lobotomies. (24 marks)

10 (a)   Describe Piaget's theory of cognitive development. (12 marks)

  (b)   Examine the evidence on which this theory is based. (12 marks)

11   Discuss biases in psychology. (24 marks)

12   'The use of vivisection is barbaric, serves no useful purpose and can never be justified in a civilised society.'

Discuss the use of non-human animals in psychological investigations. (24 marks)

Answers

1   The syllabus for Social cognition (1.1) identifies the fundamental attribution error and the self-serving bias only as examples; therefore they cannot be used as the focus points of questions in this way.

2   There is no injunction. Shame, otherwise entirely faithful to the syllabus.

3   There is no connection between the two halves of the question as they are taken from two different sub-sections of the syllabus (Social influence, and Pro- and anti-social behaviour).

4   Pavlov is not named on the syllabus. Consequently it is quite possible that candidates might have covered only more recent work in the field of classical conditioning and only encountered Pavlov as a 'historical acknowledgement'.

5   As 'consider' is a Skill A-only injunction, there is no Skill B component to the question.

6   There are three problems with this question. First, it is rather lightweight (an outline of stress and just one piece of research); second, it would almost certainly not be thought appropriate to allocate 12 marks to an outline injunction requiring just one thing (and a definition at that); and third, 18 marks of the marks are allocated to Skill A.

7   What an odd concoction: motivation in the first half of the question, emotion in the second; physiological theories in the first half, non-physiological theories in the second; and one or more in the first half, two in the second. A real ragbag!

8   The opposite to question 6 – despite being entirely faithful to the wording of the syllabus, the candidate is being asked to do far too much here.

9   Two problems: first, ECT and lobotomies are not named at all on the syllabus, so whilst it is perfectly fine for the candidate to include them in an essay on somatic treatment the examiner cannot directly ask for them. Second, the injunction – criticise – is Skill B only.

10   Two problems here: first, Piaget is named on the syllabus only as an example, so part (a) could not be set; second, the injunctions in both (a) and (b) are Skill A only.

11   This question is too vague and does not give the candidate sufficient guidance and direction. The wording in the syllabus (sub-section 7.2, Controversies in psychology) is far more helpful: 'biases in theory and research, including those relating to cultural diversity and gender'.

12   Poor selection of quotation. It focuses only on vivisection, whereas the question is on animal research in psychology *per se*, and the negative and emotive tone is unlikely to encourage candidates to write balanced and analytical answers.

How did you do? 12 out of 12? Excellent!

If not, check them through again carefully and make sure you can understand the logic behind their disqualification. It's quite interesting and helpful to have a go at actually writing your own 'wrong questions' – try it if you want.

Summary

- A number of misconceptions are held about AEB A-level psychology exam papers.
- It is *not* true that there is a pattern to the way in which questions 'come up' in different years.
- It is *not* true that some parts of the syllabus are banker topics and others are marginal. All are equally weighted.

- It is *not* true that the actual wording of questions is relatively unimportant and that 'general' answers will do.
- An understanding of why certain questions *cannot* be included on the exam paper will give you an insight into why certain others *can*.

3

Reading the questions

This is not one of the longest sections of the book, but it is one of the most important. It concerns a skill which will be vital to your exam success, but the reason I have not placed it in the (next) chapter which is concerned with maximising your performance on the Big Day of the exam is simply because it is a skill which you will need to practise and rehearse well in advance.

I still recall quite vividly my first training conference as a teacher of A-level psychology (even though it is now a rather depressing number of years ago). It was held at Lewisham College in South London, and the then-Chief Examiner, John Radford, gave a rather splendid address to the gathering on how we could develop exam performance as a skill in our students. Given that this was the mid-1970s (oh dear, that's blown my cover), it predated general concern about skills development – very much a millennium concern with all the talk of 'key skills' these days – by over a decade and a half. Radford argued that good exam performance was a skill that anyone could develop, just like any other skill such as learning to play a musical instrument, learning to drive a car or being good at sex. The process was:

- identify the principal components of the skill (for example, with driving, steering and clutch/brake/accelerator co-ordination are pretty important!)
- rehearse/practice
- respond appropriately to feedback on previous performance

(the last two points being an on-going interactive loop).

I am confident that the ability to analytically read exam questions can be developed in this manner.

The Blue Peter answer

For many years I was convinced that the reason why many candidates did not respond appropriately to what I believed were quite simple and transparent requests made by exam questions, was the Blue Peter syndrome (that is, 'here's one I made earlier', with candidates simply rewriting their 'greatest hits' essays under exam conditions). Older and a bit wiser, I now believe that it's because a large number of candidates have never been shown how to take an exam question apart, and to appreciate what it is asking them to do.

Let's contextualise this issue in a game of consequences.

What will the consequences be for the candidate who writes a general, 'all-purpose' answer to a question? How much will they lose compared to the candidate who can respond exactly to the demands of the question?

Okay, I've kept you waiting long enough. The magic formula is very simple.

Divide the question up by the separate requirements, and then identify the injunctions and the content areas linked to each of them.

Sounds simple, but it is so effective. Let's explore it through examples and our 'general' essay writer.

Types of question

The simplest form of question is:

Single injunction, single content

For example:

> Discuss the effects of the media on anti-social behaviour. (24 marks)

This question could hardly be more straightforward. The candidate needs to demonstrate both Skills A and B as defined by the injunction 'discuss' (refresh your memory of how this is defined by looking back to page 6 in Chapter 1 if you wish) with reference to one content area: 'the effects of the media on *anti*-social behaviour'. I suppose the only way our 'all-purpose answer' candidate could get this wrong would be to unbalance Skill A or B, or to focus on Pro- (as opposed to anti-) social behaviour (or perhaps to write a general essay on anti-social behaviour with little or no reference to media effects).

Not much in it so far, so let's move on to the next level of complexity.

Double injunction, single content

> Describe and analyse alternative approaches to classifying normal and abnormal behaviour. (24 marks)

We still have one content area, 'classifying (ab)normal behaviour', but there are now two injunctions: describe (Skill A) and analyse (Skill B). At this point some of you may be tempted to say that it's all very well but 'discuss', in the first example, is A + B, as is 'describe and analyse', so what's the difference?

The answer lies in the Skill B requirement. Look back at the definitions of the injunctions given in Chapter 1 (pages 5–6). Notice that 'discuss' requires you 'to describe and to evaluate…', but 'evaluate' is quite different to 'analyse': 'evaluate' requires you to make an '*informed judgement* regarding the *value* of (*x*)…', whereas 'analyse' requires you to demonstrate 'understanding through consideration of the *components or elements* of (*x*)…' (emphases added). I hope you can now see that these are quite different requirements. How will our 'all-purpose general answer' candidate do here? Not very well I suspect, because the Skill B delivery will probably be insufficiently focused.

Single injunction, double content

> Discuss one theory of cognitive development and its practical applications to education. (24 marks)

It is not unreasonable to suppose that our general-answer candidate will offer their pre-prepared Piaget answer (this is the usual case). As I have mentioned earlier it is not at all unusual in cases such as these for candidates to describe Piaget's theory, then critique it and – almost as an afterthought – tag on a couple of paragraphs (often less!) for the applications to education requirement. Such a candidate may end up getting, say 10 or 11 marks for the first discussion (the theory) and perhaps only 2 or 3 marks for the second discussion (applications to education). From glory to disaster within the space of one answer.

Finally,

Double injunction, double content

> Describe two research studies of obedience, and assess what insights these studies have given us into the nature of independent behaviour. (24 marks)

I suspect that our general-answer candidate will be all at sea here because he or she will almost certainly be offering *the* Milgram answer we discussed a little while ago. The consequences are even worse here than with the general Piaget answer above. In the first instance the requirement is to offer two studies, and the odds are that only the classic 1963 Milgram study will be given (although the Hofling *et al.* study may be given an odd paragraph). So only half marks can be gained from this requirement, in all likelihood. All of the evaluation and critiquing of Milgram which will inevitably follow the description will earn nothing because the requirement is only to 'describe'; all of the Skill B marks are for an assessment of what the obedience studies tell us about independent behaviour. Let's be absolutely clear about the consequences of this. It means:

Requirement	Response	Adequacy
one obedience study (Skill A)	Milgram 1963	probably superb
second obedience study (Skill A)	paragraph on Hofling	basic/limited
———	critique of Milgram	irrelevant
insights into independent behaviour	the odd sentence	rudimentary/basic

This candidate, having written what might otherwise be a superb Milgram answer will probably end up with around 8 or 9 marks out of 24 – in most years a fail mark.

I trust this will show you that you must be able to take questions apart so that you know just how to structure your answer. The general, all-purpose answer will not do!

Putting the Blue Peter answer to rest

This is a good time to put the Blue Peter answer in its place. Examiners call it this because there is every reason to suppose that it has been almost wholly written in advance and simply regurgitated in the exam situation ('here's one I made earlier'). In recent years examiners have witnessed the frightening spectacle of the Centre Blue Peter where almost all the candidates have reproduced, almost literally word-for-word, the same answer.

I'll not mince my words: *this is an absurdly risky practice*. I grant you that on the *odd occasion* these candidates may 'fall lucky' because the wording of the question more or less exactly fits the one that they have learned off by heart. But, as we have seen above, it only takes a little change in wording to completely alter the focus and balance of the answers required. Examiners are totally unsympathetic to candidates answering their own questions rather than those questions given on the paper, so please be warned.

The parted question

Parted questions occur throughout the exam paper, but there is no way of knowing in advance just where and in what form. As I'm sure you will appreciate, this 'air of uncertainty' makes the Blue Peter approach even more risky! I have given plenty of examples of parted questions in Appendix B, but I would now like to make clear a few points relating to them.

Skills A and B are always split into 12+12 marks (except in Research Methods). Two-part questions are already split, so the 12/12 allocation can be achieved in two ways:

(a) *Describe* two mating strategies used by non-human animals. (12 marks)
(b) *Assess* the influence of these two mating strategies on either social organisation or parental care. (12 marks)

[June 1998]

and

(a) *Discuss* some assumptions of one psychodynamic orientation in psychology. (12 marks)
(b) *Critically consider* the contributions of this orientation to two different areas of psychology. (12 marks)

[January 1998]

The key thing to note here is that in the first 12/12 question part (a) is exclusively Skill A and part (b) exclusively Skill B, whereas in the second question, Skills A and B are in both parts (a) and (b) (equally weighted, of course). Do ensure you check for this in the exam itself.

The most frequently given split other than 12/12 is 6/18. You might want to have a look at examples of these in Appendix B now. The important thing to remember is that because of the equal weighting of Skills A and B, you can work out the balance of your 18-mark answer in the following way (let's take a specific example):

(a) Outline social or cultural variations which have been found in language. (6 marks)

(b) Discuss how social and cultural variations in language influence the way in which we think. (18 marks)

Look at the injunction for the 6-mark part: it's 'outline', which is Skill A only. This means that 6 marks of the 12 available in total for Skill A have been 'used-up'. Consequently we now know that part (b) – with a Skill A+B injunction (discuss) and carrying 18 marks – will be weighted 6 marks to Skill A and 12 to Skill B. *Consequently around two-thirds of this part of the answer should be 'skill-B-ing'.*

You need to be alert to having to make the same judgements on 6/6/12, 6/12/6 and 12/6/6 questions although these are usually easier because each part tends to be either Skill A or Skill B rather than an unbalanced combination of A and B like the 6/18 questions.

Remember what I said earlier about the importance of *practising* this question-reading skill. I suggest you now spend a little time working through some (or all if you wish!) of the illustrative questions given in Appendix B.

Review exercise

Summary

- You need to be able to develop the skill of analytically reading exam questions.
- Like the development of any other skill, you need to identify the principal components of the skill, to rehearse and to respond appropriately to feedback.
- In reading questions you need to identify the skill requirements (by the injunctions) and the content.

- This is particularly important when you are answering parted questions as the focus of the question often 'shifts'.
- Once again the inappropriateness of the 'general' answer is demonstrated.

4

Doing well in the exam

At the beginning of the last chapter I argued that we can regard good exam performance as a skill – like learning to ride a bike, for example. Remember that I said (following the sound advice of one of the past Chief Examiners, John Radford) that as with any skill what you need to do to ensure success is to:

- identify the key components of the skill
- rehearse and practise these
- respond appropriately to feedback

In this chapter I will discuss factors which you need to practise and develop before the Big Day and those which are particularly pertinent to the exam situation itself.

This may sound obvious, but remember that good success means getting high marks on the day. At present in A-level psychology that means around an average of 16 marks (out of 24) in each of your answers to just get into the grade-A band, around 12 marks to just make C and about 8 marks to secure an E (based on the June 1997 statistics). These figures vary slightly from year to year. Do remember, though, that these figures are achieved in the exam environment, i.e. when you are extremely anxious, have no books or notes at your disposal, have to respond immediately to questions you have never seen before and are probably overdosed on polo mints. Not the same as your user-friendly class essays, okay?

How great Olympic athletes perform clearly depends not only factors relating to the day of the finals themselves but also to their build-up and preparation. The greatest skill and motivation in the world is no use to someone who is out of shape and under-trained. So let's begin with the 'hard slog' – our equivalent of training – building up to exam day.

Before the exam

Notwithstanding what I just said, one of the key aspects to exam success is *motivation*. However you achieve it, you have really got to want to succeed. Preparation is hard work, sometimes boring, and demands a high degree of 'stickability'. At least you don't have get up at 4 o'clock each morning to run the streets, as boxers have in the past, but you will have to make some sacrifices. Your brilliant and exhilarating social life is probably going to have to go on hold for at least a few months if you want to have a serious chance of getting high grades. Whereas effort can be misplaced (high effort/little gain) I'm afraid there is no substitute for the effort itself.

As with successful diets, the secret lies in not giving in to temptation when your resistance is low. But enough of the metaphors, let's get specific.

Attitude: Want to succeed! Need to succeed!

One student told me that the way she 'got herself on track' was to pin a blown-up photograph of the university she really wanted to go to on her wall, with a small picture of herself stuck on the steps of the main building! All I would add here is that there is nothing either I or anyone else can do for you here. Attitude has just got to come from within yourself. Parents' encouragement and cajoling is no substitute for the real thing.

So, by whatever means it takes, *get attitude*!

Your strengths and weaknesses

I've talked earlier about analysing the components of the skills you will need to master, but this, of course, is only half of the story. Your success (or otherwise, but don't let's even contemplate that!) will be a result of what is needed of you and your ability to deliver it. So *your* skills etc. obviously come into the equation too.

In our culture we are often brought up to be modest and self-effacing ('oh no really, you're too kind…' – or something like that) but what I want you to do here requires blunt self-honesty.

Take two pieces of paper. On one, list what you think are all of your strengths; on the other, list your weaknesses (continue over the page if necessary!). Some of the items will have no relevance to your study success at all (for example, nice hands, good personal hygiene) but many will, even if they are general traits and characteristics such as perseverance and determination. Others, such as being bone-idle or thick as a brick, pose a few problems (only joking with the examples, of course).

What you need to do is twofold. First, ensure that you hold on to your strengths – in trying to change themselves for the better, people sometimes throw out the good with the bad. Second, you need to see what you can do to turn-around your weaknesses. Don't be afraid to ask if you can talk these things over with your teacher or lecturer; they often have the 'distance' and lack of close personal involvement that friends lack, and their judgements in situations such as these are often better for that.

Take a careful look back at your past successes and failures

In what exams have you done well in the past? Which ones have been a disappointment? Whilst it is water under the bridge to a certain extent, it is equally true that we can learn a lot from our past.

Look at your essay marks, take the trouble to read the comments really carefully and ask what you can do to address them. Honesty and a commitment to do well are vital again here – if you are dismissive or defensive you will learn very little. Be big enough to take criticism and respond to it.

Do remember though that GCSEs, for example, and A-levels are very different beasts (more emphasis on depth of knowledge and evaluation/analysis in A-level for instance), so you're not going to be comparing like with like.

Draw up a study timetable (and stick to it!)

I was recently at a conference where one of my colleagues asked the students there if any of them were 'sad enough to have a revision timetable'. A bit of a laugh, but a serious area of concern nevertheless.

I've deliberately avoided using the term revision and have used the term study instead. This is because there is an unfortunately widespread misconception which regards revision and last-minute panic cramming as synonymous – they're not. Revision is literally re-visiting or re-seeing things we have already encountered. More of revision strategies shortly. Let's return to the timetable.

You need to determine how much time you realistically have at your disposal. Once lessons, lectures, tutorials, etc. have been taken out of the pot, how much 'spare time' do you have at school or college? What other commitments make demands on your time? Just what is left over, and where does it occur?

Certainly in the run-up to the exam you must try to make the very best use of whatever time you *do* have at your disposal. But I'm not advocating that you try working round the clock. There are two obvious reasons for this. First, you need to have energy in the exam: it will be draining both physically and intellectually. You're not going to be doing yourself any favours if you're like death-warmed-up on the Big Day. Second, Skinner was right – we all respond well to rewards. Just a few little breaks and 'treats' make life far more bearable when the pressure gets intense. It has often been said about child-care that one hour of quality time is better than hours of impoverished or uncaring contact. Much the same may be true of quality-revision.

A word of warning though. Don't take this argument too far – I'm not advocating an intensive bust of twenty minutes a day, and resting-up for the remainder!

Active revision

Innumerable psychological studies have clearly demonstrated the advantages of active rather than passive learning. One of my colleagues conjured up a wonderful image when she described a desperate student as 'reading the words on the page so intensively that they would be burned into their brain'! It just doesn't work like this.

Never just read and never try to learn material off-by-heart, parrot-fashion. The exam is for thinking human beings, not our feathered friends.

Make notes all the time, and remember that you are working *with* your materials:

- actively
- critically
- constructively

By *actively* I mean that you are interacting with the material, endeavouring to get your head around it rather than get it into your head (these are two very different goals). Understanding will never let you down in the exam, rote learning probably will. It's as simple as that.

By *critically* I mean that you should always be questioning. Phil Banyard, a Chief Examiner with another Board, advises that you always ask questions such as 'How do they know that?' Try not to just take things at face value. Might the outcome of the study have been different had the study been carried out in a different country or using different participants? How does it relate to other studies or theories? Are there any different ways the results could have been interpreted?, etc.

By *constructively* I mean that you are constantly re-drawing and re-fashioning what you are working with. Look to make links, both within topics and across different topics. Don't try to learn things in big 'linear' chunks (for example, pages 7–15 of your textbook). Be on the lookout for novel links and different perspectives. Always work with information in small 'chunks' so that you can move it around. Use cards rather than notepads, and experiment with cut and paste if you work on a computer. If you lack confidence in what you produce, your teacher or lecturer will almost always be glad to give it a quick check-over.

Getting it out as well as getting it in

Most misconceived notions of revision focus exclusively on getting facts stuffed into the head and holding them there long enough for them to tumble out in the exam room. All that I have just said about the inappropriateness of literal recall should make it clear that this is wrong. You must work *with* the information, not just 'splurge' it onto the exam paper. Furthermore, such misconceptions take no account of rehearsing *performance*.

Two very useful strategies to help you rehearse and develop performance are *planning* and *mock exams*.

Working with examples of questions taken from the list I have given in Appendix B (at the back of this book) and with copies of past exam papers (available at your school or college, or directly from the AEB) just draw up as many plans as you can. Explore different ways to answer the same question, move material around to see what 'fits' best, and so on. Try this both with and without your notes, etc. by your side. But *never* fall into the trap of deciding that one particular essay plan is the best and 'learn it' as your exam answer. Please remember what I said earlier about all the problems associated with the Blue Peter answer.

Mock exams are obviously far more demanding than drawing up essay plans, but it is important to rehearse for the real thing, so I would advise you to set yourself as many mocks as you can in the immediate run-up to the exam. You will almost certainly be set these anyway by your teacher/lecturer, but while I can't pretend that it's a case of the more the merrier(!) I can assure you practice does make perfect. Okay, enough clichés.

I accept that it is unlikely that these mock papers will be marked – I dread to think what my colleagues will be thinking regarding the implications for their workloads! – but I am confident that after reading Chapter 5 in this book you will be able to competently and confidently mark your own exam papers (no! not the real ones – I don't think the Board will allow us to go *that* far).

The exam itself

The first point to make is that there will have been no point in putting in all the hard work and developing those winning skills in the run-up to the exam if you don't put these into practice on the day of the exam. An obvious point, perhaps, but I have heard many a dejected student say that knew just what they *should* have done, but panicked in the heat of the moment and fell back into all their old bad habits. Remember to keep your nerve – if you have worked hard, know your stuff and bear in mind what I have told you in this book, you will do well.

There is a story told about a famous English batsman who, upon being wished good luck on his way to the crease, replied 'Luck has nothing to do with it madam – it's skill'. The same is certainly true here. So don't forget:

Bring forward your exam skills and use them

Just as we talked earlier about getting the right mental attitude, so it is just as important in the exam to have the right mental 'set'. I'm not going to patronise you here by saying that on the day you need to be fired up yet thinking clearly (and all the other pitifully obvious remarks that many study skills books trot out) – I'm assuming that you will be sufficiently highly motivated to have all these things in place. What I do want to concentrate on for a little while, is:

Goal orientation

By this phrase I mean that throughout the exam you need to have the object of the exercise clearly in your mind. The best way I know how to explain this is by using an analogy. Imagine a visit to your doctor. You go into the surgery, sit down and describe the symptoms of your illness or injury to the doctor, who then mentally brings all their knowledge and experience to your particular problem and offers the best advice that they can. Sounds simple, right? This is just the orientation that you should have in the exam, except this time *you* are the doctor. You need to think of the exam as a *series of problem-solving exercises*.

The equivalent of your illness is the exam questions in that they both require you to 'scroll' through all of your knowledge and skills and bring forward the ones which are *relevant to the particular situation*. If you went to see your doctor complaining of a migraine and the doctors insisted on sitting you down and telling you everything he knew about infections of the liver, you would be both surprised and displeased, and yet that's what hundreds and hundreds of students do to examiners every year.

The equivalent of the doctor's diagnosis and treatment are your exam answers: specific responses to specific demands.

Let's be quite clear about the size of the task here. If you have studied psychology for two years (or even one year intensively) you will have learned an enormous amount of psychological knowledge and acquired a wide range of skills. There is absolutely no way that two three-hour exams can do anything more than scratch the surface of this. So you must appreciate the object of the exercise is not (categorically *not*!) to see just how big a proportion you can scribble down in six hours. Believe me, size is not the issue! The wise and well-informed candidate – *you*! – will know that the object of the exercise is to *select and sample* appropriately from the 'population' of knowledge and skills that you possess. Don't be depressed at the prospect of the sample being only a small proportion, or not containing your favourite bits (that is, the questions you wanted most didn't come up) – that's just the way exams are, I'm afraid. As long as you know what the nature of the game is, you'll cope with it.

Let's finish this chapter with some specific 'bits and pieces'.

Selecting questions

Despite the guarantee of a question being set to every sub-section of the syllabus (see Chapter 1), I hope you will have been able to cover more than one per section so that you will have some choice in the exam. Remember that the questions are set down in the order that they appear on the syllabus (see Appendix A at the back of this book). So, for Social Psychology, for example, the first question will have been drawn from the Social cognition sub-section, the second from the Social relationships sub-section, the third from Social influence and the last one from Pro- and anti-social behaviour.

If you have covered more than the bare minimum of sub-sections, there will be two tasks to concern yourself with at the outset:

• selecting the questions
• analysing the requirements of the questions you select

We have dealt with the second point already (see Chapter 3) but let me spend a few minutes on the first point.

You should avoid snatching at questions, perhaps because a key word such as 'memory' leaps out at you. Remember that there is no such thing as *the* memory question or *the* ethics question. Questions are unique and specific and as such make unique and specific demands of you.

Don't necessarily pick the questions which you regard as easiest; pick the ones which will stretch you and enable you to show the examiner what you're really capable of. If you went to a concert featuring a world-class pianist you wouldn't expect her to play Chopsticks would you? If you can play the 'Rach 3', then show us your stuff!

Planning your answers

You must never 'write off the top of your head'. Essays which are unplanned are invariably chaotic, and lack shape and direction. Examiners also give credit for essays that are well structured.

Brainstorm all the remotely relevant points onto the page and then go through them and decide which ones are really relevant to answering the specific question. Be mindful of what I said about the exam being an exercise in sampling and selection. It is just as important to make good decisions about what to leave *out* as it is to decide what to include.

The next decision to make concerns sequencing. As we shall see in Chapter 5, if you just 'sling' everything at the examiner and expect him or her to sort it for you, you will do poorly. Your essay should be clearly and appropriately organised, so ordering is an important part of the planning.

Once you have selected and ordered, I suggest that you should go back to the question and draw out its demands in the form of a box such as the one below. The boxes will have different sizes and shapes according to the 'structure' of the particular question. Let's illustrate this with the following question taken from Appendix B:

(a) Define the term adolescence. (6 marks)

(b) Describe and evaluate two theories of personality change in adolescence. (18 marks)

(a)	**Skill A** Definition of adolescence	6 marks

	Skill A	**Skill B**	
(b)	Description of first theory Description of second theory	Evaluation of first theory Evaluation of second theory	18 marks

Notice how the relative size of the boxes indicate their weighting. Within each box is a brief indication of both topic and skill demanded. I suggest that having drawn up the box you then *actually write your notes into it*. This way you surely cannot fail to get the balance of the question right and respond in exactly the way which the examiner wants you to.

Beginnings, middles and ends

Psychology examiners are very conservative beasts – we like essays to have beginnings, middles and ends. However, this is not really viable for some parted questions (especially those carrying only, say, 6 marks). Once you had written an introduction and allowed for a conclusion there would be almost no time or space left for the key bit in the middle!

With the unparted, 24-mark questions you might like to consider the following formula:

• *plan of attack/outline of intent*   Here you give the examiner a brief orientation so that he or she knows what to expect. This can be very helpful to examiners as it gives them an overview of what is to follow and encourages them to 'stay with you' if you have to go into what might otherwise appear lengthy digressions. It also makes sure that *you* know what you are going to be doing before you do it. Excellent for self-discipline!

- *main body of essay* Let's sub-title this *the question answered* so that you don't lose sight of what is required of you. After 'taking out' time for reading the questions, planning your answers and checking through them at the end of the exam, you will be left with a mere thirty-five minutes or so of writing time for each answer, so you must make every sentence count. Even a single sentence wasted is a luxury you cannot afford – every one should add something to the quality of the answer. We shall examine some worked examples of this in the final chapter. Remember, *be clear, concise and focused on the question at all times*.

- *conclusion* Give the examiner a succinct summary of the main points you have raised and the main strands of your argument. This should be a review rather than simply a restating, so hold back a couple of your best summary points to put in here. Remember that you don't have to take an unequivocal stand on the topic (such as whether schizophrenia is determined more by genes than environment); it's okay to take the 'jury is still out on this one' line if you think this is appropriate.

Using your psychology

You should always bear in mind that the examination is one in psychology and the examiner will be constantly looking for evidence that you have completed a decent course in the subject (as opposed to 'spouting-off' on issues like the bar-room orator does). If I may make use of analogy again, you should think of yourself as a skilful tailor making a suit out of material which has been given to you by someone else. The material is the equivalent of your knowledge of psychological theories, studies, applications, etc., the making of the suit is the crafting of the material into an answer which is uniquely yours.

So, make extensive use of all the relevant psychological material you can, and try to source or reference it wherever possible. For example, if you make an assertion such as 'there have been many examples in the past of psychological studies with animals which would not be acceptable now' make sure you give some examples and make sure you say *why* they would not be acceptable today (for example, because of ethical guidelines). *Never* make grandiose statements (such as 'nobody takes Freud seriously these days') unless you can support and substantiate them, preferably by referring to a named source (for example, 'Humphreys (1999) states…'). Again, think of the tailor crafting his material.

I have tried to write this book in an informal, chatty style, almost as though I was sitting by your side helping you to prepare for the exam. But this approach is the exception rather than the rule in psychology writing and in the exam you should endeavour to write in the same style as that used in the textbooks that you have read.

Time management

Even the best students sometimes cannot stop themselves spending far too long writing on a favourite topic – they just have so much to say! But you must try to avoid this temptation. I mentioned that you only have around thirty-five minutes of writing time per question, it is important that you apportion this fairly and equally, because if you spend, say, fifty minutes on one essay, it is either 'squeezing' the other three or is robbing one of them of fifteen minutes (nearly half of its 'allocation'). Just look at the example below to see the consequences of this. In a typical year the first candidate would earn an A grade

Good candidate	Question	Mark
	1st	18
	2nd	17
	3rd	17
	4th	16
	total	68
Poor candidate	Question	Mark
	1st	22
	2nd	13
	3rd	12
	4th	4
	total	51

whereas the second would be borderline C/D, and yet the A-grader never hit the heights achieved by the other student in their first answer.

Having mentioned grades, let's now move to a consideration of just how your exam work will be marked.

Summary

- *In a typical year*, the gap between a C grade and an A grade is only 4 or 5 marks out of 24.
- *Exam preparation and performance* can be considered in terms of the period before the exam and what you do on the day itself. In terms of the first of these:
  - want to succeed
  - assess your individual strengths and weaknesses
  - try to learn from your previous successes and failures
  - draw up a realistic study timetable which has clear, achievable goals
  - always revise actively rather than trying to 'download' the book into your brain (can't be done); work actively, critically and constructively
  - plan answers and set yourself mock exams

- *On the day of the exam itself*:
  - in the heat of the moment, don't lose sight of all the skills and knowledge you have acquired
  - think of answering the questions as a problem-solving exercise
  - remember the exam can only sample a small proportion of what you know and can do
  - choose questions which enable you to really show what you are capable of – don't just go for the easy options
  - write your plans in boxes which show the balance between the skills and the content areas (see page 50 for example)
  - answers should be clearly structured with beginnings, middles and ends, and they should have direction and 'flow'
  - never waste time repeating points – try to make every sentence contribute something to the quality of the answer

- try to always substantiate your points (think of yourself as the tailor crafting the garment with material already provided)
- don't fall into the trap of spending too long on your favourite questions – remember that time is always time stolen from another question

5

Marking the answers

We have nearly reached the end of our journey, the aim of which has been to enable you to prepare yourself as well as possible for your forthcoming exam in AEB A-level psychology. All that remains now is to show you how your script will be marked by the examiner so that you will know exactly what you will need to do to pick up marks.

The marking scheme

All examiners are required to mark to a scheme which is published for general purchase *after* the exam (for obvious reasons!). The scheme is made up of two parts:

1 The first part is a question-specific section which discusses, for example, studies or theories which candidates might focus on, typical responses to the question, likely areas of difficulty, etc. Because these comments are entirely question-specific, there is no point in us dwelling on them here since the only questions you are likely to be interested in are those which will be coming up on your paper.

2 The second part of the scheme, however, is general to all questions, except Research Methods. You will recall that this section is

different to all the others in many respects (refresh your memory by having a look back at Chapter 1 if you wish). This identifies how the essay is to be marked according to the qualities it has or lacks.

These criteria are published in this book as Appendix C. So have a look now, and then come back here.

Decisions the examiner has to make

Two initial points:

1   The examiner gives *marks*, not grades. In fact they are instructed never to think in terms of grades when marking (for example, 'that seems like a C to me', or 'that one's just about worth a pass'). The reason for this is very simple: the examiners do not themselves decide what band of marks cover a B or an E for example. This decision is made *after* all the marking has been carried out and is decided by a committee at what is called an Award meeting. Nothing mysterious or sinister here, it is simply that the level of difficulty of exams may vary slightly from year to year and this needs to be taken into account when determining the grade boundaries.
2   The examiner is required to give each answer a *separate* mark for Skill A and Skill B. This is very important. What it means in practice is that one part of your answer cannot 'carry' or compensate for another. No matter how good the descriptive demonstration of your knowledge and understanding (Skill A) is, you will only be able to pick up 12 out of the 24 marks for this.

So you need to ensure that *overall* your answers are *balanced*, but remember that in parted questions you will be asked to 'do' different things in different parts of the question (see Chapter 3).

The marking criteria

You can see in Appendix C that assessment of both Skill A and Skill B is determined by reference to three criteria. For Skill A they are:

- *the quality of the psychological content* (your knowledge and understanding of theories, studies, concepts, etc.) ranging from 'just discernible, muddled, inaccurate and anecdotal' through to 'accurate and well detailed'
- *construction and organisation* ranging from 'reasonable' to 'coherent'
- *breadth/depth* ranging from 'some evidence of breadth/depth' to 'substantial evidence of breadth/depth and an appropriate balance between them'

For Skill B the criteria are:

- *analysis, assessment, criticism, evaluation, interpretation or justification as specified in the question* (this ranges from 'weak, muddled, incomplete' through to 'informed and thorough')
- *use of material* ranging from 'restricted' to 'highly effective'
- *elaboration* ranging from 'some evidence of elaboration' to 'coherent elaboration with evidence of appropriate selection'

From fail to pass and from C to A

How then can you improve your exam performance? The million-dollar question indeed.

Built onto the back of all the information and suggestions I have offered you already, here are a few final hints. Given what we now know about Skill A and Skill B being marked separately, my remarks will be directed accordingly.

For Skill A

The only angle we've not already covered is the construction and organisation criterion. The key thing here is to avoid writing essays that look like shopping lists (that is, 'here is one study, here's another and here's a third'). Make sure that your material is integrated (by which I mean interweaved into the whole fabric of the essay rather than the answer being a string of stand-alone paragraphs). Remember what I said in Chapter 4 about the need for your answers to have good shape and flow. Two little final tips here. First, try to link your paragraphs wherever possible so that the essay isn't characterised by a whole series of jolts and dramatic, unannounced changes of direction. Second, try to throw in the odd explicit statement linking what you are saying directly back to the wording of the question. This always shows the examiner you are 'on track' and conscious of adapting your material and skills to the demands of the specific question.

For Skill B

Whenever the display of skills is badly imbalanced in an answer it is almost always Skill B which is lacking. So let's see what we can do about this.

With regard to the first criterion given on the marking scheme, ensure that you are displaying the appropriate aspect of Skill B. All the way back in Chapter 1 we looked at the differences between analysis, assessment, evaluation and so on. As I have said before, always try to make sure that you can substantiate any criticisms that you make with evidence or sourcing.

Remember what I said about being able to use contrasting studies (or theories) as a *counter-point* to the one you are describing for Skill B. This will broaden your Skill B delivery considerably.

Perhaps the final point I want to make about strengthening your Skill B is the most important one. It concerns both the use of material and the elaboration criteria.

By highly effective *use of material* we mean that you are able to really extract the maximum 'mileage' out of what you know. We have all heard, I'm sure, about brilliant lawyers who can win a case even when working with only the most flimsy evidence (conversely there are others who would struggle to clinch the case if it fell down and died in front of them!). This is what we mean by use of material. One of the best ways to make by far the best use of material is by *elaboration*. You will get some credit for one-liners such as 'a criticism of Freud is that he was sexist', but think about how much better it is if it is elaborated. Try the formula:

1   Describe the criticism.
2   Give an example of it.
3   Assess the appropriateness of the criticism.

For example

> One criticism of Freud is that his work was sexist: that is, it tended to be both written from a male point of view and saw women as generally inferior or 'less than' men. One example of this bias would be his idea of penis envy, which Freud also tied to what he believed to be females' inferior morality. However, in his defence it should be pointed out that Freud was writing in Victorian times when views about the differences between men and women were very different to those in our culture today. Furthermore, feminist writers such as Juliet Mitchell have re-analysed Freudian psychodynamic theory and have argued that even after the so-called sexist elements are removed there is still much left which is creditworthy.

Better than 'Freud was sexist', or what?!

Chapter 6 follows with samples of student answers from other titles in this textbook series (thanks all!). Remember that all the books in the series contain worked examples of student essays with advice on how they can be improved.

In conclusion may I wish you the very best of luck in the exam. Oh no, I forgot – luck has nothing to do with it, it's skill! Let me, then, wish you good skill.

Summary

- All answers except those for Research Methods questions are marked according to specific criteria – these are given as Appendix C at the end of this book.
- Examiners always award marks rather than grades.
- Skills A and B are assessed separately.
- Skill A is judged on the quality of the psychological content; construction and organisation; and breadth/depth.
- Skill B is judged on the quality of the analysis, assessment (etc.); use of material; and elaboration.
- A series of final tips is given on how to convert a C grade into an A.

Practice essays from the series

Please note that marks given by the examiner in the practice essays should be used as a guide only and are not definitive. They represent the 'raw marks' given by an AEB examiner. That is, the marks the examiner would give to the examining board based on a total of 24 marks per question broken down into Skill A (description) and Skill B (evaluation). Tables showing this scheme are in Appendix C at the book of the book. They may not be the marks given on the examination certificate received ultimately by the student because all examining boards are required to use a common standardised system called the Uniform Mark Scale (UMS) which adjusts all raw scores to a single standard acceptable to all examining boards.

Practice essay 1

(a) Explain what psychologists mean by the term *cognitive development*. **(6 marks)**

(b) Discuss *two* theories of cognitive development. **(18 marks)**

Starting point: In this essay part (a) is entirely description ('explain').
Part (b) consists of both description and evaluation, though the

'description' component is smaller (6/18 marks), the evaluation is worth 12 out of 18 marks.

Candidate's answer

(a) A child's cognitive development is the way they change their thinking as they grow up. For example, when a young child is shown a row of counters being spread out they think there are more counters because they do not understand conservation. As the child gets older they realise that quantity doesn't change.

Examiner's comments

The answer covers the basic points and gives a reasonable example with some detail. Therefore we could describe it as appropriate but limited. It would receive about 4 out of 6 marks. If the example had been more clearly explained or elaborated the mark would be higher, as it would had the initial definition included further points beyond the Piagetian view of cognitive development. For example, cognitive refers to more than just thinking: it includes all mental activities such as beliefs, imagery, memory and so on.

Candidate's answer

(b) I will discuss Piaget's and Vygotsky's theories of cognitive development. Piaget divided development into four stages. The first stage is called the sensorimotor stage. It is when the infant is learning to co-ordinate incoming sensory data with motor actions. The infant is born with certain innate reflexes or schema, such as a sucking reflex. This enables them to interact with the world and gradually build up more complex schema. Around the age of nine months the child develops object permanence. This is when (s)he realises that, if an object is out of sight it still exists. Before this age the child does not realise this.

The end of the sensorimotor period is marked by the onset of language, at about the age of two. This child now moves into the pre-operational stage and can use symbols such as language and numbers. This stage is subdivided into the pre-conceptual period (2–4 years) and the intuitive phase (4–7 years). The child's thought processes do not use the same logic as adults. This is shown by things such as animism, the tendency to give inanimate objects animate characteristics, such as thinking that a chair can be sad. Pre-school children also show egocentric thought, as shown by Piaget's classic three-mountains experiment where children could only imagine the view from their position. They are also unable to conserve. Piaget conducted a series of experiments to demonstrate this. For example, he showed children two identical rows of counters and asked if both rows had the same number of counters. He then spread out one of the rows and asked whether both rows still had the same number of counters. Children in the pre-operational stage think the spread out row has more counters. He did the same with volume (beakers) and mass (balls of clay). Older children are able to conserve and know that quantity doesn't change even though it may look bigger.

The third stage is called concrete operations. In this stage the child is beginning to use more adult-like logic, but cannot operate on abstract concepts. For example when asked if 'Tom is taller than Susan, Tom is smaller than Jack, who is tallest?' a 6-year-old can answer but not if they were asked the same thing in symbolic form ('A is greater than B, A is less than C, is B greater than C?').

The last stage of development is called formal operations which starts from the age of about eleven. At this age children can now use abstract adult thought. Their reasoning is systematic and organised. Some people have questioned whether all adults do have this kind of thought, and suggest that Piaget was wrong to think that this is a universal stage.

A key element of Piaget's theory is that he thinks all these changes are due to maturation. Piaget thought that there is no way you could train a 4-year-old to use formal operations because his or her mind is simply not ready. As the brain matures, children develop qualitatively different kinds of thinking. Piaget said that you are born with certain invariant cognitive structures: assimilation and accommodation. A person of any age first tries to assimilate any new experience within existing schema. If this is not possible disequilibrium is created and the person must accommodate their existing schema, that is to develop new ones to fit the new experience. In this way schema, operations and knowledge develop. These schema and operations are called variant intellectual structures because they change as we get older.

The second theory of cognitive development is Vygotsky's. He suggested that children's thinking develops more because of cultural (social) influences than because of innate factors. Children are born with elementary mental functions and this can only be turned into higher functions such as problem solving through the influence of 'experts', that is people with more knowledge. Some of this knowledge is transmitted through language but experts also directly teach children. Vygotsky's key concept was the zone of proximal development (ZPD) which is the distance between a child's current and potential ability. Instruction is critical in waking those abilities lying dormant in the ZPD. This is different from Piaget's view because he thought that as soon as a child was ready (s)he would move forward.

Examiner's comments

The description of Piaget's theory is very competently done. It is appropriate, accurate and well detailed, displaying a good level of knowledge and understanding. Note the use of examples to explain the points that have been made. What is missing is empirical evidence (evaluation) and commentary/analysis (also evaluation). This means that even though it is a very knowledgeable answer, the mark will not be high because it is largely descriptive. It is also unbalanced. When a question asks for two theories, a candidate must include two in order to get full marks. The brief mention of Vygotsky is helpful but not sufficient for top marks for the descriptive part of the question. Part (b) would only receive around 4 out of 6 marks for description because of this lack of balance.

There is some evaluative material included in the answer: some empirical evidence, one brief criticism and one comparison of the two theories. At best this could be described as a 'restricted, superficial and rudimentary' and as such would be credited with about 4 out of 12 marks. Note that empirical evidence is not always evaluative material. It may be used in its own right rather than being used to appraise something, and then counts as description or narrative.

The total mark for the whole question would be around 12 out of 24 marks, likely to be a grade C at A level. You can see from this answer that the problem is time. Everything that has been included is relevant but there simply is not time to include all of this *and* the evaluative material which is critical for a better mark. Turning a grade C answer into grade A is not just a question of adding material but is also a question of removing it, removing things which are irrelevant or chat. In an exam, a student must be selective and must include both description and evaluation. Examiners are aware of what is possible within the time limit and do not expect more than this. They are looking for a good balance.

How could this answer be improved? The candidate clearly should be a bit more familiar with a second theory of cognitive development. More importantly, however, the candidate needs to offer detailed and effective analysis. This could have been done through the use of more empirical evidence (for and against both views), criticising the theory (for example, Piaget tends to overlook social influences) and/or suggesting ways that the theory could be applied. You can also evaluate a theory by offering a contrasting viewpoint, as was done very briefly at the end of this essay. A small amount of evaluative material would easily have lifted this essay to a grade B.

Practice essay 2

Discuss the use of two cognitive-behavioural therapies in the treatment of psychological disorders. (24 marks)   [AEB 1998]

Starting point: 'Discuss' is a term which requires the candidate to both describe and evaluate the two chosen therapies. The description needs to detail the ways the named therapies are used, and can include the rationale behind them, the techniques involved and the disorders they are used to treat. The evaluation can include a discussion of how effective the therapy is (as shown by outcome research, for example), as well as how ethical it is (for example, the extent to which control is exerted by the therapist) and how practical it is (for example, cost-effectiveness, availability).

Candidate's answer

Cognitive behavioural therapies were founded by Ellis, believing that with the correct help, thoughts, feelings and beliefs could be rationalised with the help of a trained therapist. The concept then developed of Rational Emotive Behavioural Therapy (REBT), a technique devised believing that cognition and behaviour play a part in evaluating. Anxiety, stress and depression are all thought to be psychological disorders. Cognitive therapies help to identify the source relating to the particular symptom, then help to alleviate it.

The ABC model devised by Ellis would be one such strategy. Here the client is shown a programme. The client and therapist then work through this programme identifying where ideas could be perceived differently. The plan is made up of: A – Activating Event; B – Beliefs about A; C – Consequences of B. The activating event could be 'sitting a psychology exam'. Beliefs could either be positive ('have tried and maybe next time revise and work a little harder') or negative thoughts ('I'm no good at this, I should have taken biology'). The consequences then depict the thoughts we felt previously, 'there is always another time' or 'I shall finish college'.

Meichenbaum and Cameron also devised a programme (stress inoculation programme) which consists of three components: conceptualisation; skills training and rehearsal; application and follow-up. Conceptualisation is to help identify the particular source of stress. Stress training and rehearsal deals with alleviating the stress, identifying the skills necessary in dealing with the stressor, and practising such strategies. And finally application is applying such techniques in a relaxed and therapeutic environment, where help is available if any problems arise.

Therapies such as those mentioned above do of course work if the patient/client is able to self-evaluate. Patients with schizophrenia who have lost touch with the real world would find these therapies difficult. In about 70 per cent of patients undertaking any behavioural therapy the findings are that they are effective, although the critics would say that there are too many variables to be valid.

These programmes such as Ellis' and Meichenbaum and Cameron's have been used in a variety of settings: NHS, Social Services and work places (stress management). Although not as cheap and as quick as somatic treatments (that is, drugs, ECT), they are seen to have no serious side-effects. Unlike psychodynamic approaches where the patient has to be in the best of health to undergo regression, these concentrate on cognitions and behaviour, helping patients to help themselves. As with all therapies, maybe an eclectic approach would be the answer.

This essay is well-structured in terms of having a clear introduction, a description of the two therapies and an evaluation section. It starts well with an explanation of the basis of cognitive-behavioural therapy, although little detail is provided and there are some inaccuracies. For example, the descriptions of Ellis's REBT and Meichenbaum's Stress Inoculation approach are clear if limited and lacking in depth. The evaluation section makes some sound points, but they could be better elaborated and the range of issues discussed could be broadened. No outcome research is presented, which is a serious omission in a question of this nature.

The final mark for this question is about 12–14, which is likely to be equivalent to a grade C at A level. What the candidate presents is generally accurate, but lacks detail. To improve on this, more information needs to be included on techniques used in such therapies, for example, the use of 'homework' and 'thought-stopping', and the ways in which these techniques are underpinned by cognitive-behavioural theories. Ethical and practical considerations could be included, as could outcome studies such as that of Clark (1992). These outcome studies can in turn be criticised. With questions of this type, the candidate needs to bear both parts of the question in mind when selecting which therapies to discuss. In this case, the candidate has chosen two which can be described fairly well, but are not associated with any specific evaluation – just general comments about cognitive-behavioural therapy.

Practice essay 3

Discuss why the assessment of personality and intelligence tests by means of psychometric tests might be considered controversial applications of psychology. (24 marks) **[AEB 1998]**

Starting point: The essay can be broken down into three smaller questions to answer:

(i) *How has psychology attempted to measure personality and intelligence?*

(ii) What are the positive arguments for measuring intelligence and personality?

(iii) What are the negative arguments?

Part (i) is description and Parts (ii) and (iii) are evaluation.

These are the issues that need to be addressed, and the answer needs to identify the areas of controversy and say why they are controversial.

Candidate's answer

There are several different psychometric tests, like motivational tests, aptitude tests, personality and intelligence tests and they can be used to see whether someone is suitable for a job, have they got the right attitude to do the job and not the right qualifications. These tests can also be used to see whether the people will work well with their colleagues.

Examiner's comments: A breathless start to the essay, and a novel (if not brave) use of punctuation. It is a good idea to write in sentences (which means using full stops) and also to use short sentences. The paragraph does give a range of possible psychometric tests and says what they might be used for.

All these tests are very controversial and are widely discussed it is not just the problem of the test itself it is who is going to have access to the information should it be freely available or only available to the future employer or only the person him/herself. The results may effect the person by lowering their expectations and this could lead to problems of depression is this right and justifiable?

Examiner's comments: The poor punctuation continues throughout the essay so I will have one more moan about it and then shut up. Please write in sentences. An important issue is raised in the paragraph, namely the control of information from psychometric tests. It is raised as a question which is a good way to introduce it.

Another problem is that the tests themselves may not be a true assessment of the person, there are many different factors to take into account such as gender, cultural background, true intelligence, how much education you have had. Francis Galton did a study on Victorians and found that the wealthy families were much more intelligent and this was hereditary. The people in the slums were stupid and this was also hereditary. The problem with this is that the rich people had more education so were more likely to be intelligent.

Examiner's comments: This paragraph identifies the problem of inferring ability by testing performance. The writer, however, does not state this problem very clearly and goes on to make some alarming and only partially true assertions about Galton. It is always best to use technical terms in essays and, surprisingly enough, 'stupid' is not a technical term. On the other hand, it is worth knowing that 'moron', 'imbecile', 'cretin' and 'idiot' are, in fact, technical terms used by the early intelligence testers. This paragraph also gives the first outing to the author's rather simplistic view of genetic influences on performance.

Cultural issues are very difficult to rule out and cross-cultural psychometric tests are very hard to be bias free. One study showed that a Rail Attendants test at Paddington Station was biased against male Asians so many were not employed unfairly.

Examiner's comments: Cultural bias is certainly one the of important issues in psychometric testing, and the writer has illustrated the point with a badly remembered study.

Many tests are eurocentric and so are bias towards the White male middle class American or European. So if the test like this it is unlikely to be favourable to people who don't fit this bracket.

Examiner's comments: The term 'Eurocentric' means that the tests are constructed within the context of European ideas, attitudes and skills. It does not have anything to do with class or gender. Those are other sources of possible bias in tests.

It seems every test has a problem not to be bias even GCSE's can be bias because the British Government lays out guidelines for the syllabuses leading sometimes to controversies.

Examiner's comments: This is another reasonable point, but it could be developed much further by identifying the actual problem or by identifying the controversy.

There are a few tests that have been developed such as the Wheschler test – this has problems because it is more of a social conformity test rather than an intelligence test. Another two tests are the Alice Heim test and the British Ability Scale which by the name implies applies only to British people. Tests can also have problems discriminating about gender, some tests were done and it was found that women and girls were doing overall better than men and boys, so the results were changes so that women and girls had to get better results for the same mark. This is what they wanted to do for black people and applications of tests is this fair?

Examiner's comments: The writer correctly identifies another two tests but seems to know little more than the names of the tests. The point about adjustments to norms based on gender is appropriate though it is poorly developed.

What do you do with the results of the psychometric tests this could lead at the worst possible scenario to Eugenics and what Hitler did – trying to eradicate a race.

Examiner's comments: Adolf Hitler must be one of the most commonly cited people in psychology essays. The point is neither well made nor developed. The argument is this; if psychometric tests can be shown to measure ability rather than performance, and if differences between groups of people can be confidently identified and measured, and if these differences can be attributed to genetic influences rather than environmental ones, then it would suggest that selective breeding (eugenics) might be favoured by some people. There is a lot of 'ifs' in this argument and at least some of them need identifying in the essay.

There are two types of intelligence fluid which is innate and genetic and chrystalised which contains part of the fluid intelligence but is mainly to do with the environment. Is there a need for a complete classification of personality and intelligence? For employment it is useful so a lot of time and money is not spent on training someone who is not suitable for the job. Other areas of use which are personal will remain in discussion.

Examiner's comments: The first point is partially true and marginally relevant. The second point about the need for testing is a little more relevant but does not directly address the question.

Overall the writer shows a reasonable amount of psychological knowledge and identifies a few of the controversial issues around psychometric testing. Unfortunately, the knowledge is a little sparse and the points are only developed quite weakly. The expression is also quite weak. The final mark for this question is about 7 (description) + around 6 (evaluation) = 13/24 (likely to be equivalent to a grade C at A level).

Practice essay 4

Describe and evaluate research into the effects of any *two* drugs on behaviour. (24 marks) **[AEB 1997]**

Candidate's answer

The two drugs I am going to describe and evaluate are iproniazid, an antidepressant, and chlorpromazine, an antipsychotic tranquilliser.

There are two types of depression. One type is reactive depression and this occurs when we suffer a trauma such as the death of a close relative. The other form is endogenous depression and this is the depression that can be considered to be abnormal as it occurs in the absence of any traumatic event.

The cause of depression is believed to be an underactivity of monoamines which are a type of neurotransmitter substance. The monoamine neurotransmitters consist of noradrenaline, dopamine and serotonin.

Iproniazid is a MAOI. It works at the synapse. The synapse is a region where the terminal bouton of one neuron meets the dendrites of the next neuron. In between there is a small gap called the synaptic cleft. The terminal bouton has vesicles in it which contain the stored neurotransmitter. When an action potential comes along the axon the neurotransmitter is released into the cleft and travels to receptor sites on the dendrites. Here it causes ion channels to open and this results in either an EPSP or an IPSP.

Monoamine oxidase (MAO) is an enzyme that breaks down monoamine neurotransmitters and so a monoamine oxidase inhibitor (MAOI) stops MAO from working. As iproniazid is a MAOI it has this effect. By doing this it enables the neurotransmitter to work for longer and so it reverses the underactivity of monoamines in a depressed person.

Iproniazid is a very good antidepressant although it does have a number of side effects associated with it. These side effects can be quite bad. It is therefore not always used and an alternative is a tricyclic antidepressant. This does the same thing but does it differently and with fewer side effects. Iproniazid takes quite a long time to work and so ECT can be used in the meantime.

Schizophrenia is a mental disorder in which a person suffers from delusions, disordered thinking, and hallucinations. The delusions can either be delusions of grandeur in which the person might think that they are God, or delusions of persecution in which they might think that the police are after them. The hallucinations associated with schizophrenia are usually auditory rather than visual.

The cause of schizophrenia is believed to be an overactivity of dopamine. This is referred to as the dopamine hypothesis of schizophrenia. Chlorpromazine stops the overactivity of dopamine. It does this by blocking the receptor sites for dopamine and so prevents it from working.

Like iproniazid, chlorpromazine has rather bad side effects. It can also cause Parkinson's disease with prolonged use. It can also cause tardive dyskinesia. This fact is not consistent with the dopamine hypothesis of schizophrenia.

Overall, the two drugs discussed are good for helping to relieve the behavioural problems of depression and schizophrenia. However, neither of them are magic bullets and so one could criticise their use.

Examiner's comments

At first glance this looks like a very competent answer. However, the essay suffers from a very common fault. It does not answer the question very well. It is true that the answer is packed with mostly accurate information but if we analyse it paragraph by paragraph you will see where this candidate falls down. Note, though, that the candidate does not present any studies. This is perfectly acceptable as the term research includes theory, of which there is mention in the essay. Note also that physiological events are acceptable as demonstrations of behaviour.

The first paragraph is fine and accurate. The second paragraph is quite knowledgeable but is not relevant to the essay. The examiner will therefore ignore it. The third paragraph is good but there is no detail here. Where, for example, is this underactivity?

The first sentence of the next paragraph is OK but the rest of the paragraph is, at best, overlong. There is no real need here to describe the structure and function of the synapse in detail. The next paragraph is very good and would earn good credit. The last paragraph on iproniazid is not wholly accurate. Iproniazid is only a moderately good antidepressant. ECT is not generally used unless absolutely necessary. The rest of that paragraph is good evaluation but is lacking in detail. What are the side effects? Where do tricyclics act? Why do they have fewer side effects?

Overall, the first part of the answer is too descriptive (of which much is not wholly relevant). The evaluation is very limited.

For chlorpromazine the first paragraph is knowledgeable and accurate but is, unfortunately, not relevant. The second paragraph is good but the candidate ought to have indicated where in the brain this overactivity occurs. This could then be mapped onto the behavioural symptoms that are manifest.

The evaluation is again very thin and not entirely accurate. It is only Parkinson's-like symptoms that develop. What are the side effects? Why is tardive dyskinesia not consistent with the dopamine hypothesis (although not wholly relevant, anyway)? What behaviours are changed with the use of the drug? What other drug options are there? Are there non-drug solutions that are side-effect free?

The last paragraph is quite insightful. Unfortunately, the candidate does not tell us what a magic bullet is.

The final mark for this question is about 8 (description) + around 4 (evaluation) = 12/24 (likely to be equivalent to a grade C at A level).

Appendix A

Analysis of the AEB syllabus

1 SOCIAL PSYCHOLOGY

1.1 Social cognition

Activity/ process	Content	Specific focus	Including	For example
theories; research studies	influence of social factors upon perception		social identity theory; social representation; cultural identity	
	attribution theory		errors; biases	fundamental attributional error; self-serving bias
	stereotypes (social and cultural); prejudice; discrimination	origins; maintenance		
	prejudice; discrimination	reduction		

1.2 Social relationships

Activity/process	Content	Specific focus	Including	For example
theories	interpersonal relationships			reinforcement and need satisfaction; exchange theory
explanations; research evidence	interpersonal relationships	formation; maintenance; dissolution		
components of	interpersonal relationships			goals and conflicts; power; roles
nature of	relationships	individual, social, cultural diversity		
effects of	interpersonal relationships			happiness; mental health

1.3 Social influence

Activity/process	Content	Specific focus	Including	For example
research	conformity; obedience; independence			
theories; research	social power		leadership; followership	
explanations; research evidence	collective behaviour		crowds; mob behaviour	

1.4 Pro- and anti-social behaviour

Activity/ process	Content	Specific focus	Including	For example
explanations; research studies	altruism; bystander behaviour			
social-psychological theories	aggression			social learning theory; social construc-tionism
implications of research	aggression	reduction and control of aggressive behaviour		
	pro- and anti-social behaviour	media influences		
explanations	pro- and anti-social behaviour	individual, social, cultural diversity		

2 COMPARATIVE PSYCHOLOGY

2.1 Evolutionary determinants of behaviour

Activity/ process	Content	Specific focus	Including	For example
evolutionary explanations	behaviour of non-human animals			
nature of	competition for resources		exploitation; resource defence	
effects of	evolution of behaviour patterns	predator– prey and symbiotic relationships		

2.2 Reproductive strategies

Activity/ process	Content	Specific focus	Including	For example
nature and consequences	sexual selection in evolution		mate choice; mate competition	
	differential investments of males and females	rearing of the young		
influence of	social organisation; parental care	mating strategies		
evolutionary explanations	parent– offspring conflict			

2.3 Kinship and social behaviour

Activity/ process	Content	Specific focus	Including	For example
genetic explanations	apparent altruism			
	sociality in non-human animals		social co-operation as a means of defence and attack in predator–prey relation-ships	
nature consequences	imprinting; bonding	in precocial species; in altricial species		
explanations	use of different signalling systems in non-human animals			communica-tion in marine mammals

2.4 Behaviour analysis

Activity/ process	Content	Specific focus	Including	For example
theories; procedures	classical conditioning; operant conditioning			
explanations	learning in the natural environment		foraging; homing behaviour	
research	animal language			studies of natural animal language; attempts to teach human language to non-human animals
evolutionary explanations	human behaviour		limitations of these explanations	

3 BIO-PSYCHOLOGY

3.1 Basic neural and hormonal processes and their influences on behaviour

Activity/ process	Content	Specific focus	Including	For example
	organisation, structure, functioningof CNS, ANSand endocrine systems		interactions between CNS, ANS and endocrine systems	
influences	physiological, behavioural functions	CNS; ANS; endocrine systems	homeostasis	
	neural and synaptic activity			
research (on effects)	drugs and behaviour			

3.2 Cortical functions

Activity/ process	Content	Specific focus	Including	For example
investigation	cortical functioning	methods and techniques used		
research	localisation of function		sensory and motor processes; hemisphere asymmetries; split brain	
	visual perception	structure and processes involved	relevance of neurophysio-logical explanations of perceptual phenomena	

3.3 Awareness

Activity/ process	Content	Specific focus	Including	For example
research	bodily rhythms; states of awareness	physiological and psychological factors associated with	sleep; dream states	
research	sleep	nature functions		
theories; research studies	hypnosis			

3.4 Motivation, emotion and stress

Activity/ process	Content	Specific focus	Including	For example
research	brain systems; motivation; emotion	relationship between		
theories (physiological, psychological)	motivation; emotion			
theories; research findings	effects of stress on the body		relationship between stress and illness	
methods	stress reduction			biofeedback; anxiolytic drugs

4 ATYPICAL DEVELOPMENT AND ABNORMAL BEHAVIOUR

4.1 Atypical development

Activity/ process	Content	Specific focus	Including	For example
theories; research	learning difficulties	major causes; problems		
research	physical and sensory impairments	psychological effects	coping with physical sensory impairments	
theories; research	emotional behavioural problems in childhood adolescence	causes and effects of		ADHT; autism; developmental dyslexia

4.2 Conceptions and models of abnormality

Activity/ process	Content	Specific focus	Including	For example
defining; classifying	normal and abnormal behaviour	DSM; ICD	practical problems; ethical implications	
assumptions	models of abnormal psychology	medical; behavioural; cognitive; humanistic; psychody-namic	implications for treatment; ethical implications	
definitions	abnormality	cultural, subcultural differences	biases in classification and diagnosis	

4.3 Psychopathology

Activity/ process	Content	Specific focus	Including	For example
description; explanations	abnormali-ties; psychological disorders	genetic/ neurological and social/ psychological contributions	schizo-phrenia; depression; anxiety disorders; eating disorders (including their symptoms)	phobias; PTSD (for anxiety disorders)

4.4 Therapeutic approaches

Activity/ process	Content	Specific focus	Including	For example
treatment; therapies	psychological disorders	appropriate-ness; effectiveness	therapies: behavioural, cognitive-behavioural, humanistic, psychody-namic, somatic	
	therapy intervention	ethical issues		informed consent; confiden-tiality; choice of goals

5 COGNITIVE PSYCHOLOGY

5.1 Perceptual processes

Activity/ process	Content	Specific focus	Including	For example
theories; explanations	perception		constructivist; direct theories	Gregory; Gibson
	perceptual development + methods of study			
	perceptual organisation		space; movement; pattern recognition; perceptual constancies; illusions	
	perceptual organisation	individual, social, cultural variations		

5.2 Attention and performance limitations

Activity/ Process	Content	Specific focus	Including	For example
theories; evidence	focused attention: auditory, visual			
theories; evidence	divided attention			
nature; research evidence	automatic processing			
theories; research	performance deficits		action slips; dual task limitations	

5.3 Memory

Activity/ process	Content	Specific focus	Including	For example
theories; research	nature of memory		structure; processes; types of memory	
explanations	memory	organisation of information		
explanations	forgetting			
practical applications of research	memory forgetting			eye-witness testimony; memory for medical information

5.4 Language and thought

Activity/ process	Content	Specific focus	Including	For example
theories; research findings	language acquisition	process of		
explanations; research findings	production; comprehension of language			speaking/ writing; listening/ reading
models; explanations	human thought			reasoning; decision making
theories; evidence	language and thought	relationship between		
	relation of language to thought	social and cultural variations		

6 DEVELOPMENTAL PSYCHOLOGY

6.1 Early socialisation

Activity/ process	Content	Specific focus	Including	For example
theories; research	process of social development	early years	development of sociability attachments	
theories; research	effects of enrichment and deprivation	on the child		
research	child-rearing	culturally-specific aspects; cross-cultural differences	effects of	

6.2 Cognitive development

Activity/ process	Content	Specific focus	Including	For example
theories; evidence	(models of) cognitive development			Piaget; Vygotsky; information processing
practical applications	research into cognitive development			classroom practices
factors associated with	development of intelligence test performance		genetic and environ-mental influences	

6.3 Social behaviour and diversity in development

Activity/ process	Content	Specific focus	Including	For example
theories; evidence	moral development	theories: SLT, psychodynamic, cognitive-developmental		
theories; evidence	development of gender	SLT; psychodynamic; cognitive-developmental		
theories; evidence	development of the self	SLT; psychodynamic; cognitive-developmental		

6.4 Adolescence, adulthood and old age

Activity/ process	Content	Specific focus	Including	For example
theories; research	adolescence	personality change; social development		Erikson; Marcia
theories; research	adulthood	personality change		Erikson; Levinson
	adjustment to old age			disengagement; activity theory
research	life events in adulthood			parenting; divorce; bereavement; unemployment

7 PERSPECTIVES

7.1 Approaches to psychology

Activity/ process	Content	Specific focus	Including	For example
assumptions; contributions	major theoretical orientations in psychology		approaches: behaviourist, humanistic, psychody-namic	
debates in psychology	nature of the person		free will and determinism; reductionism	

7.2 Controversies in psychology

Activity/ process	Content	Specific focus	Including	For example
'controver-sial' applications	psychological research		advertising; propaganda and warfare; psychological testing (including personality intelligence testing)	
arguments	psychology as a science	for and against		
	psychological theory research	biases	cultural diversity; gender	

7.3 Ethical issues in psychology

Activity/ process	Content	Specific focus	Including	For example
	ethical issues in psycholog- ical research	research with humans; attempts to resolve above	development and role of ethical guide- lines	
	use of non- human animals in psychological investigations	constraints on using animals + arguments for and against use of animals	development and role for conduct of animal research	
	ethical responsibili- ties	wider social issues	socially sensitive research; issues of social control	'alternative' sexualities; race
	responsibility of researcher	sensitivity to social cultural diversity		

Appendix B

Illustrative exam questions

A necessary disclaimer

The questions which follow are merely illustrative of those which can be set insofar as they are consistent with general guidelines which question-setters work to (see Chapter 1) and those which have been set to date (June 1998). They are solely my own suggestions and have not been seen or approved by the AEB. There is no suggestion whatsoever that any of these questions will appear on future exam papers. The questions are primarily to give you an indication of how parts of the syllabus might be examined, but you are referred to copies of past exam papers which may be purchased for a modest sum from: The Publications Department, Associated Examining Board, Stag Hill House, Guildford, Surrey GU2 5XJ.

In what follows I have generated a large number of specimen questions for each sub-section of the syllabus, questions which, I hope, illustrate the different styles which can be used by the question-setters in examining the syllabus. Those of you of a creative bent may like to 'cross-reference' by applying all the different styles of questions to the syllabus areas you are studying. Having now read the contents of this book, such a task should prove relatively easy for you.

SOCIAL PSYCHOLOGY

Social cognition

A   Compare and contrast social identity theory and social representations as theories of the influence of social factors upon perception. (24 marks)

B   (a) Explain what is meant by social identity theory. (6 marks)
(b) Describe one research study carried out into social identity theory. (6 marks)
(c) Assess the extent to which social identity theory is an adequate explanation of the influence of social factors upon perception. (12 marks)

C   (a) Outline one attribution theory. (6 marks)
(b) Critically consider the extent to which this theory enables us to understand errors and biases in the attributional process. (18 marks)

D   Distinguish between two theories of attribution. (24 marks)

E   (a) Define the terms prejudice and discrimination. (6 marks)
(b) Discuss psychological insights into either the origins or the maintenance of prejudice and discrimination. (18 marks)

F   Discuss the origins and maintenance of social and cultural stereotypes. (24 marks)

G   Critically consider psychological work that has endeavoured to reduce prejudice and discrimination. (24 marks)

H   Discuss the extent to which our understanding of the nature of prejudice and discrimination might be used to help us reduce them. (24 marks)

Social relationships

A   Compare and contrast two or more theories of interpersonal relationships. (24 marks)

B   Critically consider the extent to which psychological theories have helped us understand interpersonal relationships. (24 marks)

C   Discuss research evidence relating to the formation of interpersonal relationships. (24 marks)

D   Critically consider psychological explanations of the dissolution (breakdown) of interpersonal relationships. (24 marks)

E "No man is an Island, entire of itself." (John Donne)
   Describe and assess what psychologists have shown to be the main components of the relationships we have with others. (24 marks)

F Critically consider what psychologists have found out about the components of relationships (e.g. goals, conflicts and rules that characterise their lives together). (24 marks)

G (a) Describe the social and cultural variations that have been found to exist in relationships. (12 marks)
   (b) Assess the consequences of these variations. (12 marks)

H 'Psychology has too long been focused upon the loves and lives of American college students as an easy alternative to researching the rich diversity of relationships which exist world-wide.'
   Discuss. (24 marks)

I Critically consider what psychologists have shown us to be the effects of interpersonal relationships (e.g. on happiness and mental health). (24 marks)

J Discuss the view that interpersonal relationships are one of the major contributors to the quality of our lives (e.g. our mental health and our happiness). (24 marks)

Social influence

A (a) Describe two research studies of either conformity or obedience. (12 marks)
   (b) Assess what these studies have told us about the nature of independent behaviour. (12 marks)

B With reference to specific research, distinguish between conformity and obedience. (24 marks)

C (a) Explain what psychologists mean by the term social power. (6 marks)
   (b) Critically consider how studies of leadership have shown this to be a form of social power. (18 marks)

D Describe and evaluate two theories of leadership or followership. (24 marks)

E Discuss two or more ways in which psychologists have explained collective behaviour (for example crowd or mob behaviour). (24 marks)

F   "Collective behaviour, especially crowds and mobs, has been the subject of much empirical and theoretical research (but no one theory) appears to offer a completely adequate account..." (McIlveen, 1998)
    Discuss. (24 marks)

G   Write the Milgram answer. (100 marks) – ONLY JOKING!!

Pro- and anti-social behaviour

A   (a) Explain what is meant by the term altruism. (6 marks)
    (b) Discuss one study which has been made of either altruism or bystander behaviour. (12 marks)
    (c) Assess what this study has told us about the nature of altruism. (6 marks)

B   Compare and contrast two theories of altruism. (24 marks)

C   (a) Define the term aggression. (6 marks)
    (b) Describe one social-psychological study of aggression. (6 marks)
    (c) Critically consider two social-psychological theories of aggression. (12 marks)

D   (a) Describe two or more social-psychological theories of aggression. (12 marks)
    (b) Assess the implications of two of these theories for the reduction and/or control of aggression. (12 marks)

E   Critically consider the extent to which it has been shown that the media exerts a pro-social influence on behaviour. (24 marks)

F   (a) Describe one psychological study of pro-social behaviour. (6 marks)
    (b) Describe one psychological study of anti-social behaviour. (6 marks)
    (c) Assess the extent to which social and cultural diversity have been found in either pro- or anti-social behaviour. (12 marks)

COMPARATIVE PSYCHOLOGY

Evolutionary determinants of behaviour

A   Critically consider the adequacy of evolutionary concepts as explanations of the behaviour of non-human animals. (24 marks)

B (a) Describe two or more ways in which animals have been shown to compete for resources. (12 marks)

   (b) Evaluate the effectiveness of these strategies. (12 marks)

C Critically consider what exploitation and resource defence have told us about the nature of competition for resources. (24 marks)

D Discuss the effects of predator–prey and symbiotic relationships on the evolution of behaviour patterns. (24 marks)

E (a) Briefly explain what is meant by either predator–prey or symbiotic relationships. (6 marks)

   (b) Critically consider the insights which the study of predator–prey and symbiotic relationships have given us into the evolution of behaviour patterns. (18 marks)

Reproductive strategies

A Discuss the nature and consequences of sexual selection in evolution. (24 marks)

B Describe and evaluate mate choice and mate competition in terms of their consequences for sexual selection. (24 marks)

C Critically consider two or more explanations for the differential investment shown by males and females in the rearing of the young. (24 marks)

D (a) Discuss the influence of mating strategies on social organisation. (12 marks)

   (b) Discuss the influence of mating strategies on parental care. (12 marks)

E "Before the 1970s sexual reproduction was usually seen as a way of perpetuating the species through the cooperative behaviour of two individuals….The focus now is on the individual organism that desperately attempts to achieve its ends through a mixture of aggression, advertising, deceit, trickery and double standards." (Cartwright, 1996)

   Critically consider the extent to which research in comparative psychology supports the contemporary view given above. (24 marks)

F (a) Explain what is meant in comparative psychology by parent–offspring conflict. (6 marks)

   (b) Critically consider the adequacy of evolutionary explanations for parent–offspring conflict. (18 marks)

Kinship and social behaviour

A   Describe and evaluate genetic explanations for apparent altruism. (24 marks)
B   Critically consider social co-operation as a means of defence and attack in predator–prey relationships. (24 marks)
C   (a) Explain what is meant by the terms imprinting and bonding. (8 marks)
     (b) Critically consider the extent to which research has shown imprinting and bonding to be similar and/or different to each other. (16 marks)
D   Discuss the view that imprinting is different to all other forms of learning. (24 marks)
E   (a) Consider two signalling systems used by non-human animals. (12 marks)
     (b) Assess the advantages and disadvantages of these two systems. (12 marks)

Behaviour analysis

A   Distinguish between classical and operant conditioning. (24 marks)
B   (a) Discuss the procedures used in classical conditioning. (12 marks)
     (b) Discuss the procedures used in operant conditioning. (12 marks)
C   Describe and evaluate two or more explanations of either foraging or homing behaviour. (24 marks)
D   Discuss research which has been carried out into animal language, for example studies of natural animal language and/or studies of attempts to teach language to non-human animals. (24 marks)
E   Describe and criticise evolutionary explanations of human behaviour. (24 marks)

BIO-PSYCHOLOGY

Basic neural and hormonal processes and their influence on behaviour

A   Discuss examples of the ways in which it has been shown that the central nervous system, the autonomic nervous system and the endocrine system interact with each other. (24 marks)

B   (a) Describe the structure of the autonomic nervous system. (12 marks)

     (b) Assess the influence of this system on behavioural functions (e.g. homeostasis). (12 marks)

C   (a) Define the term homeostasis. (4 marks)

     (b) Describe the influence of the autonomic nervous system on homeostasis. (8 marks)

     (c) Assess the influence of either the central nervous system or the endocrine system on behavioural functions. (12 marks)

D   Discuss how neural synaptic activity occurs and the processes which are involved in this activity. (24 marks)

E   Describe and evaluate research into the influence of drugs on behaviour. (24 marks)

Cortical functions

A   (a) Describe two or more methods/techniques which have been used to investigate cortical functioning. (12 marks)

     (b) Evaluate the strengths and weaknesses of these methods. (12 marks)

B   Describe and evaluate research which has been carried out into brain asymmetries. (24 marks)

C   Discuss research into localisation of function in the brain. (24 marks)

D   Critically consider the relevance of neurophysiological explanations of perceptual phenomena. (24 marks)

E   (a) Describe the structure and processes involved in visual perception. (12 marks)

     (b) Assess the extent to which visual perception can be understood in terms of its neurophysiological basis. (12 marks)

Awareness

A Describe and critically assess research into either sleep or dream states. (24 marks)

B (a) Describe two bodily rhythms (6 marks)

  (b) Discuss research which has demonstrated either physiological or psychological factors involved in bodily rhythms. (18 marks)

C Discuss research which has been carried out into the functions of sleep. (24 marks)

D (a) Explain what is meant by the term hypnosis. (6 marks)

  (b) Outline and evaluate two theories of hypnosis. (18 marks)

Motivation, emotion and stress

A Critically consider the relationship between brain states and motivation and/or emotion. (24 marks)

B (a) Explain what is meant by the term emotion. (6 marks)

  (b) Describe and evaluate one psychological theory of emotion. (12 marks)

  (c) Assess what this theory has told us about the nature of emotion. (6 marks)

C Compare and contrast physiological and non-physiological theories of motivation. (24 marks)

D (a) Describe one theory of stress. (6 marks)

  (b) Discuss research which has examined the effects of stress on the body. (18 marks)

E Describe and evaluate methods used to reduce stress, for example biofeedback and anxiolytic drugs. (24 marks)

ATYPICAL DEVELOPMENT AND ABNORMAL BEHAVIOUR

Atypical development

A 'Coping with physical impairments involves not just physical demands but, perhaps more significantly, psychological ones as well.' Discuss. (24 marks)

B   Describe and assess two or more theories relating to the major causes and problems associated with learning difficulties. (24 marks)

C   Discuss theories and/or research relating to the causes and effects of emotional problems in childhood. (24 marks)

Conceptions and models of abnormality

A   (a) Describe two or more approaches to defining abnormality. (12 marks)

(b) Assess the ethical implications of these approaches. (12 marks)

B   (a) Describe either the DSM or ICD classificatory system. (12 marks)

(b) Assess practical problems associated with classification of abnormal behaviour. (12 marks)

C   (a) Outline the assumptions of the behavioural and psychodynamic models of abnormal psychology. (12 marks)

(b) Assess the implications for treatment of one of these models. (12 marks)

D   "All the things that we take for granted (about normality) are not set in stone. For every 'normality'…has been shown to be otherwise at different periods in history and in different parts of the world." (Humphreys, 1997)

Critically consider cultural and subcultural differences in the definition of abnormality. (24 marks)

Psychopathology

A   Critically consider the contribution of genetic/neurological factors to schizophrenia. (24 marks)

B   (a) Describe the symptoms of two anxiety disorders. (6 marks)

(b) Discuss the contribution of either genetic/neurological or social/psychological factors to these one of these anxiety disorders. (18 marks)

C   Describe and assess the contribution of social/psychological factors to eating disorders. (24 marks)

Therapeutic approaches

A Compare and contrast humanistic and cognitive-behavioural therapies for psychological disorders. (24 marks)

B (a) Describe the main features of either the psychodynamic or somatic treatments for psychological disorders. (12 marks)

   (b) Either justify or criticise one of these treatments in terms of its effectiveness. (12 marks)

C Discuss ethical issues involved in therapy and intervention. Such issues might include informed consent, confidentiality and the choice of goals. (24 marks)

COGNITIVE PSYCHOLOGY

Perceptual processes

A Distinguish between constructivist and direct theories of perception. (24 marks)

B (a) Describe two or more methods which have been used to study perceptual development. (12 marks)

   (b) Assess the strengths and weaknesses of these methods. (12 marks)

C In 1890 William James described the perceptual world of a young baby as "a blooming, buzzing confusion". Discuss the extent to which psychological research into perceptual development has supported or challenged this view. (24 marks)

D Describe and evaluate psychological research into perceptual organisation (e.g. space, movement, perceptual constancies, visual illusions). (24 marks)

E Describe psychological research into individual, social and cultural variations in perceptual organisation, and assess the extent to which this research enables us to determine whether the world looks the same to everyone. (24 marks)

Attention and performance limitations

A (a) Explain what is meant by focused attention. (6 marks)

   (b) Discuss two studies of either focused visual or focused auditory attention. (12 marks)

    (c) Assess the extent to which these studies can give us insights into the nature of attention. (6 marks)

B   Describe and evaluate two theories of divided attention. (24 marks)

C   Consider and analyse what research evidence has told us about the nature of automatic processing. (24 marks)

D   Describe and assess theories of action slips and dual task limitations. (24 marks)

E   "Can we do two things at once? As so often in psychology, this is a simple question but the answer is anything but simple." (Eysenck, 1997).

Discuss psychological research relating to this statement. (24 marks)

Memory

A   Critically consider psychological research relating to different types of memory. (24 marks)

B   Describe and assess research findings relating to the nature of memory. (24 marks)

C   Discuss explanations of how information is organised in memory. (24 marks)

D   (a) Discuss two psychological explanations for why we forget. (12 marks)

    (b) Critically consider practical applications of these explanations. (12 marks)

E   Describe and assess practical applications of psychological research into memory and forgetting. (24 marks)

Language and thought

A   Compare and contrast two theories of language acquisition. (24 marks)

B   Critically consider what psychological research has told us about either the production or the comprehension of language. (24 marks)

C   Examine and evaluate two theories which have been forwarded to explain human thought. (24 marks)

D "Human beings…are very much at the mercy of the particular language which has become the medium of expression for their society. We see and hear and otherwise experience very largely as we do because the language habits of our community predispose certain choices of interpretation." (Sapir, 1941)
Discuss. (24 marks)

E (a) Outline social or cultural variations which have been found in language. (6 marks)

(b) Discuss how social and cultural variations in language influence the way in which we think. (18 marks)

DEVELOPMENTAL PSYCHOLOGY
Early socialisation

A (a) State what psychologists mean by the terms attachments and sociability. (6 marks)

(b) Describe one study of social development in the early years of life. (6 marks)

(c) Criticise the study you have just described. (6 marks)

(d) Assess what the study has told us about the process of social development. (6 marks)

B Describe and assess psychological research into the development of attachments and/or sociability. (24 marks)

C "Not everyone is convinced that it really is possible to accelerate development in young children. In the past, influential experts…insisted that development is largely a matter of maturation and unfolding, and that there is no point in encouraging early learning.… Parents and others should simply wait until a child is 'ready' to move forward." (Howe, 1995)
Critically consider whether research into the effects of early enrichment supports the above view. (24 marks)

D (a) Describe research into cross-cultural differences in child-rearing. (12 marks)

(b) Assess the effects of these differences. (12 marks)

Cognitive development

A   (a) Outline one theory of cognitive development. (6 marks)

      (b) Critically consider the extent to which research evidence has supported this theory. (18 marks)

B   Distinguish between two theories of cognitive development. (24 marks)

C   Describe two theories of cognitive development and assess their practical applications to education. (24 marks)

D   Critically consider the influence of genetic and environmental factors on intelligence test performance. (24 marks)

Social behaviour and diversity in development

A   Compare and contrast the psychodynamic and cognitive-developmental theories of moral development. (24 marks)

B   (a) Explain what is meant by the term gender. (4 marks)

      (b) Outline two theories of gender development. (8 marks)

      (c) Assess what these theories have told us about the nature of gender. (12 marks)

C   (a) Describe two theories which have been forwarded to explain the development of the self. (12 marks)

      (b) Assess the evidence on which these theories are based. (12 marks)

D   Discuss ways in which psychological research has helped us to understand the development of either moral or gender development. (24 marks)

Adolescence, adulthood and old age

A   Discuss psychological research into social development in adolescence. (24 marks)

B   (a) Define the term adolescence. (6 marks)

      (b) Describe and evaluate two theories of personality change in adolescence. (18 marks)

C   Describe and evaluate two theories of personality change in adulthood. (24 marks)

D   "Popular culture is geared towards younger people. Which is odd, because, for example, there are far more people aged over 50

in Europe than there are teenagers. How, then, are older people expected to respond to a world that is apparently against catering for their needs?" (Stuart-Hamilton, 1997)
Critically consider how research into the ways people adjust to old age helps us answer this question. (24 marks)

E   Describe and evaluate psychological research into the effects of life events in adulthood (e.g. parenting, divorce, bereavement, unemployment). (24 marks)

PERSPECTIVES

Approaches to psychology

A   Discuss the contributions to psychology of behaviourism and psychodynamics. (24 marks)

B   Discuss the assumptions made by any two major theoretical orientations in psychology (e.g. the behaviourist, humanistic and psychodynamic approaches). (24 marks)

C   (a) Consider some of the main issues in the free-will versus determinism debate. (12 marks)
    (b) Analyse examples of this debate within psychology. (12 marks)

Controversies in psychology

A   Critically consider why applications of psychological research in psychometric testing (e.g. measurement of intelligence and personality) could be considered controversial. (24 marks)

B   Critically consider arguments for and against psychology being classified as a science. (24 marks)

C   'Throughout most of its history psychology has been concerned with men rather than women and white people rather than people of other colour.'
    Discuss. (24 marks)

D   Consider and analyse alleged biases (such as gender and race) that have characterised psychology research and/or theory. (24 marks)

E   Outline and assess any two psychological theories in terms of their gender or racial bias. (24 marks)

Ethical issues in psychology

A   (a) Describe ethical issues which have been raised in psychological research. (12 marks)

       (b) Assess attempts which have been made to resolve these issues. (12 marks)

B   "Many of the ethical considerations that apply to humans (such as informed consent and privacy) could not apply to non-human animals. Researchers have almost absolute power over their subjects, and thus the risks of taking part in research may be far greater for animal subjects than they would be for their human counterparts." (Cardwell, 1997)

With reference to specific studies, discuss the role of ethical guidelines in the conduct of psychological research with non-human animals. (24 marks)

C   Discuss the case for and against the use of non-human animals in psychological research. (24 marks)

D   "How can we engineer a social consent which will make people behave in a socially adaptive, law-abiding fashion?...The psychologists would answer that what was clearly required was a technology of consent – that is, a generally applicable method of inculcating suitable habits of socialized conduct into the citizens (and preferably the future citizens) of the country in question – or preferably the whole world." (H.J. Eysenck, 1969)

Discuss issues arising out of psychological research relating to social control (24 marks)

E   Discuss the responsibilities of psychologists to be sensitive to social and/or cultural diversity in their work. (24 marks).

Appendix C

Marking criteria used in AEB A-level and AS-level psychology

Skill A assessment criteria

Band	Marks	Psychological content	Construction/ organisation	Breadth/ depth
1 bottom	0–2	just discernible, muddled, inaccurate, anecdotal	——	——
1 top	3–4	basic, rudi-mentary, sometimes flawed	——	——
2 bottom	5–6	limited, generally accurate but lacking in detail	reasonable	some evidence of
2 top	7–8	limited but accurate and reasonably detailed	reasonable	increasing evidence of
3 bottom	9–10	slightly limited, accu-rate and well detailed	coherent	evidence of both but imbalanced
3 top	11–12	accurate and well detailed	coherent	substantial evidence of both and appropriately balanced

Skill B assessment criteria

Band	Marks	Analysis, evaluation, etc.	Use of material	Elaboration
1 bottom	0–2	weak, muddled, incomplete	——	——
1 top	3–4	minimal, superficial, rudimentary	restricted	——
2 bottom	5–6	reasonable but limited	reasonably effective	some evidence of
2 top	7–8	reasonable but slightly limited	effective	evidence of coherence
3 bottom	9–10	informed	effective	coherent with evidence of appropriate selection
3 top	11–12	informed and thorough	highly effective	coherent with evidence of appropriate selection

Skill D (QoL) assessment criteria

Band	Marks	Expression of ideas	Use of specialist ideas	Grammar, punctuation, spelling
1	0	poor	limited range	poor
2	1	adequate	good range	adequate
3	2	accurate	precise/broad	only minor errors